THE THERAPY ANSWER BOOK

THE THERAPY ANSWER BOOK

Getting the Most Out of Counseling

Kathleen J. Papatola, Ph.D.

Fairview Press   *Minneapolis*

Published by Fairview Press, 2450 Riverside Avenue South, Minneapolis, MN 55454.

Library of Congress Cataloging-in-Publication Data
Papatola, Kathleen Joan, 1952–
    The therapy answer book: getting the most out of counseling / Kathleen J. Papatola
        p.   cm.
      Includes index
      ISBN 1-57749-048-7 (alk. paper)
        1. Psychotherapy--popular works.   2. Consumer education.
  I. Title.
  RC480.515.P36   1997   97-30506
  616.89'14--dc21   CIP

First Printing: November 1997

Printed in the United States of America
01 00 99 98 97   7 6 5 4 3 2 1

Jacket design: Laurie Duren

Publisher's Note: Fairview Press publishes books and other materials related to the subjects of social and family issues. Its publications, including *The Therapy Answer Book,* do not necessarily reflect the philosophy of Fairview Health Services.

For a free current catalog of Fairview Press titles, please call 1-800-544-8207, or visit our website at www.press.fairview.org.

This book is dedicated to my friend J. F. Powers
with deepest affection and gratitude.

CONTENTS

ACKNOWLEDGMENTS

A heartfelt thank you to those who so kindly and graciously supported me:

To my husband, Tim Peterson, whose enduring patience, humor, intelligence, and creativity were a constant source of energy and hope.

To my children, who lent a whole new meaning to the word "humble."

To my parents, Dorothy and Joseph Papatola, for their life-long support and belief in who I am.

To friends and colleagues who generously gave their time, ideas, feedback, and enthusiasm for this project: Kathy McKay, MS, LP; Rick Mons, MBA; Michael Scott, PsyD, LP; Charles A. Peterson, PhD, LP; and Ed Bonnie, PhD.

Special thanks to the people at Fairview Press:

Lane Stiles, Senior Editor, for his enthusiasm for the project, willingness to help in any way he could, and belief that all things are possible.

Stephanie Billecke, for the hours of critical reading, thoughtful editing, suggestions, and organization.

Dan Verdick and Gayle Callistro, for their delightful energy and creativity.

Kevin Lovejoy, for thinking of me in the first place.

INTRODUCTION

My supervisor walked into the office and handed me a chart at least three inches thick. "I've got a new patient for you," he said, smiling. "She's a challenge, but I think you're up to it."

"Great!" I said. (Newly minted PhDs don't say no to their supervisors.) I glanced at the mammoth chart. "Are you sure?"

"Not a doubt in my mind."

A few days later, I ushered the patient into my office and began asking her some questions about herself. She was the oldest child from a very accomplished family. Bright. Hospitalized three times for manic-depression and twice for alcoholism. A couple of serious suicide attempts. Longstanding problems with bulimia—there were days when she did nothing but eat and throw up. Overweight. Chain smoker. Occasional hallucinations.

The patient was twenty-nine-years old. My age.

She was a great storyteller—colorful and animated. After listening to her speak in riveting detail for half an hour, I found myself thinking, "Good Lord, you need help! You should see somebody." Then it dawned on me. She *was* seeing somebody, and that somebody was me.

It was a humbling moment.

Fifteen years and hundreds of patients later, this patient still crosses my mind every now and then—usually when I start feeling too cocky for my own good.

People seek help from mental health professionals because they hurt, and they want the pain to go away. They look to therapists as the experts. We therapists pull out our toolboxes—carefully constructed through years of training, supervision, research, workshops, and study—and we try to find a tool to fit each problem. We work hard to help our clients help themselves.

If therapists have stumbled anywhere in our profession, it has been in our failure to educate our patients about what we do and why we do it. Instead, we savor our role as experts, and we allow our profession to remain shrouded in mystery.

The purpose of this book is to begin tugging at that shroud and educating people who are curious about therapy: clients, graduate students, teachers, and therapists themselves. It is a guide to the therapy process, written in plain English, that addresses some basic questions:

- What is therapy?
- How do you know if you need it?
- What makes a good therapist, and how do you find one?
- What are the steps in the therapy process?
- How will you know when you're done?
- What is managed care, and how do you get your insurance to pay for your treatment?

More importantly, this book will empower you to ask questions and make decisions that are right for you. It will help you get the most out of therapy.

Treatment is a partnership—a joint effort between client and therapist. Learn your part well. It's worth the investment.

CHAPTER ONE

WHAT IS THERAPY?

When Julie signed on as sales director for a new hunting and sporting goods manufacturer, she was ecstatic. Having spent the previous eight years as an associate sales director for a competitor, she was more than ready to make the move up.

The company she joined was young and aggressive; it had been touted by leading industry magazines as an organization to watch. In a business where women are seldom seen (and almost never in management), she beat out six other candidates for the position, all of them men. The president made a point of telling her how much they appreciated her, and hinted at a promising future—stock options, higher visibility, maybe even a seat on the board.

Julie is bright and organized, a no-nonsense kind of leader who is as comfortable in camouflage as she is in a Calvin Klein original.

Sales quotas for her region are aggressive—more aggressive, she thinks, than for the regions run by her male counterparts who, unlike Julie, have had trouble meeting their quotas the last two quarters.

Julie regularly puts in sixty hours a week, not counting travel time. She is known for her ability to promote new relationships with buyers and salvage old ones battered by her predecessors. She holds the line on pricing without angering her clients. She has designed some of the most successful sales contests in the company, and her once-skeptical sales force has come to accept her.

Julie is used to fielding strange looks from store managers as she advises them on product displays; she especially enjoys their reaction when she starts blowing on a duck call.

The job is becoming more stressful, though. After three years and countless hints by the president about a promising future, she has yet to be offered stock; nor has she been promoted into a more visible role of leadership.

Over the past three months, Julie has started to feel vaguely dissatisfied. Restless. Not as enthusiastic. And tired—a heavy sort of tired that doesn't go away, even with a good night's sleep. The kind of tired that siphons off her interest for new projects.

Her thrice-weekly workouts at the local sports and health club have dwindled to barely once a week, and she's stopped packing her gym clothes when she travels. She rarely socializes with friends on weekends anymore, preferring instead to settle in with a rented movie and a bowl of popcorn. Her longtime boyfriend tells her she's much more irritable and grumpy than she used to be.

Julie feels the change and she doesn't like it. She knows that unless there is a shift of some sort, it will be difficult for her to keep up with her work. She considers seeing a mental health professional to help her sort through some options, but she decides against it for now, choosing instead to do a little sleuthing on her own.

She starts with what she knows—that she's unhappy. She's not completely sure why, so she sets up a self-observation record in a notebook and keeps it with her at all times. She divides the page into two columns. The first column she titles "What Happened," the second, "My Feelings (Score)."

Julie records situations that cause her to react in the first column. In the second, she names the most prevalent feeling associated with each situation, rating the intensity of the emotion on a scale of 0 to 10, 0 being the lowest level of intensity and 10 being the highest.

Julie decides to keep her record for one month. By keeping track of her reactions to various situations at work, she can identify interactions that contribute to her unhappiness (see chart on page 4). Afterwards, she will determine what action she should take to restore her happiness.

Julie's positive feelings rated highest when she was on the road, helping members of her field force to make sales, open new accounts, and demonstrate new products. She felt satisfied, excited, competent, and enthusiastic.

Her highest negative ratings occurred at the office and were frequently related to her boss, the president of the company. Ironically, when Julie's boss commented favorably on her performance, she felt irritated, angry, and resentful.

Recognizing a pattern, Julie draws up a list of options to rectify the situation. Some ideas are more realistic than others, but generating a list gives her a feeling of power and flexibility.

What Happened	My Feelings (Score)
Helped Ray open new account (North Dakota)	Satisfied, excited (8)
Demonstrated new product to store manager (Wisconsin)	Competent (9)
Discussed new sales projections with reps (home office)	Apprehensive (5)
Introduced sales contest to reps (home office)	Enthusiastic (9)
Received memo from boss congratulating me on last quarter's results (home office)	Irritated (8)
Invited to Iowa for new store opening by buyer (e-mail)	Pleased (7)
Invited by boss to represent company at major trade show (home office)	Resentful (8)
Invited by boss to meet with major client in Bill's region, where sales have dropped by 20 percent (home office)	Angry (10)
Received excellent performance review—compensation okay, nothing on stock or promotion (home office)	Angry, resentful (10)

Options

• Spend more time on the road developing accounts and working with my sales force.

• Wait for my next performance review and have a frank conversation with my boss about my concerns. Ask about my future with the company, including the possibility of remuneration, promotion, and increased responsibility. Ask for a timetable.

• Schedule the above conversation ASAP—don't wait for the performance review.

• Look for a new position with a different company, carefully outlining my expectations and goals before deciding to move.

• Start my own company. With my experience in the industry, I could form my own sales rep group, possibly taking some of my current staff and accounts with me.

• Look for a job in a different industry altogether. The amount of travel involved in sales is difficult and tiresome, and it cuts into relationship time.

• Go back to college and get an advanced degree in business.

• Go back to college and get an advanced degree in something else.

• Cash in my retirement savings and take six months off to think about my next move.

Julie promises herself to add to this list over the next two weeks as ideas pop into her head, then take another week to decide on a course of action. For the first time in months, Julie feels like she is back in control.

———

Every year, Lisa went to the state fair with her best friend, Tracy. It was a ritual that started back in eighth grade, the summer the two of them turned thirteen. That was the summer their parents said it was okay to go alone.

They each brought $30 that year, money they saved from baby-sitting and yard work. They vowed not to come home until they were both flat broke. Making a bet to see who could eat the most, they systematically made their way through foot-long hot dogs, buttered corn on the cob, chocolate-dipped strawberries, popcorn, fudge, fried cheese curds, vanilla malts from the Dairy Barn, and the Best French Fries in the World. For the grand finale, they finished off a bucket of Sweet Martha's chocolate chip cookies and a quart of milk while sitting on the curb near the main entrance, waiting for Tracy's dad to pick them up.

That was also the year Tracy talked Lisa into riding the double Ferris wheel. The only year. Her hands still get clammy when she thinks about climbing into that bright yellow seat, watching the safety bar drop over their heads, and hearing the lock slam into place. Lisa remembers like it was yesterday—the knot in her stomach got bigger as they made their way from the top of the first wheel to the top of the second. A wave of terror washed over her when Tracy started swinging their chair back and forth. She elbowed Tracy in the ribs without turning to look at her, afraid that any movement would make the seat swing even more.

"Tracy, knock it off," she said between clenched teeth. "I hate this. I don't know why I let you talk me into this." Tracy looked at her friend's panic-stricken face, stiff body, and white knuckles frozen on top of the bar.

"Hey," she said. "Come on, it'll be okay." She laid her hand across Lisa's.

They went to the fair every year in high school. When they chose colleges in different states, they phoned and e-mailed on a regular basis and always planned summer vacations to ensure their

annual ritual. And when Real Life descended after college graduation, they were determined to carry on with their tradition. They
had ten state fairs under their belt and wondered where they'd be
after twenty.

Eventually, the food orgies gave way to science exhibits, the
forestry building, political booths, and horse shows. They stopped
occasionally to listen to a band or a barker. They reminisced about
the past and shared hopes for the future, trading stories about interesting men and dream vacations. They marveled at their busy lives.

Lisa was running late for an appointment one afternoon when
the phone rang. She almost didn't answer it, but she'd forgotten to
turn on her answering machine. Tearing through kitchen-counter
clutter, she grabbed the receiver.

"Lisa?" the voice said, tentatively.

"Yeah, who's this?"

"Lisa, it's Corrine, Tracy's mother."

"Oh, hi! How's it goin' ?"

"Lisa, something horrible has happened. Tracy's dead."

It was as if she'd been struck in the chest by a bowling ball. Lisa
couldn't catch her breath. Dizzy and light-headed, she sank into a
kitchen chair.

"What? What are you talking about? What happened?"

"We're still not sure," Corrine's voice continued steadily,
reflecting the many times she'd repeated the story. "She was out
having dinner with friends. They said she had just started eating
when she said she wasn't feeling well, that she had a bad
headache and was going to the ladies' room. She stood up, let out
a moan, grabbed her head, and passed out. They called the para-
medics right away, but she never woke up. She died before they
could get her to the hospital."

Lisa couldn't believe it. She'd just gotten an e-mail from Tracy
a couple of days ago. She hadn't even answered it yet. This wasn't
possible. Tracy was only twenty-four. The only other person she'd

known who died was her great-grandfather, but that was when she was fourteen and he was ninety-eight.

Lisa was devastated. And lost.

She served as one of her friend's pallbearers and read a short eulogy during the funeral service. When it was time to go to the gravesite, she felt like she did that day on the Ferris wheel. This time there was no one to reassure her that everything would be okay.

Lisa has spent the last six months feeling as if her life will never be the same. She cries, although less frequently now, at what she calls "the dumbest things"—the smell of food frying, songs on the radio, sunny days, rainy days, corn dogs. She visits Corrine whenever she can, and they trade stories about Tracy. She has talked at length with Tracy's friends who were with her the night she died—asking the same questions over and over again, and hearing the same answers. They share the shock and the loss. Not too long ago they all went out together, to that same restaurant, and toasted Tracy with a bottle of her favorite wine.

Even now it's hard for Lisa to check her e-mail. She knows it's crazy, but she still scans her messages for Tracy's return address.

Lisa goes to the cemetery a couple of times each month. She talks to Tracy and still tells her things she tells no one else. She leaves small baskets of flowers and always sticks in little somethings Tracy would have liked. August is coming again soon—state fair time. Maybe Sweet Martha's this time.

———

An honor-roll student since his sophomore year in high school, David was a first-string quarterback, president of the student counsel for three years, and state record holder for the mile run. He was accepted into every college he applied to, and two offered him full scholarships. After graduating with honors, David started his own computer consulting business. By all accounts, he led a charmed life.

Karen was thrilled when David asked her out. She was the first woman he had ever paid any real attention to. Although he had dated briefly in high school, he was generally uneasy among his peers. When it came to relationships, David felt clumsy and inept.

Karen and David were married after a six-month long, whirl-wind courtship. When they first started dating, she was working as a nursing assistant at the local children's hospital and David's business was booming. Karen was impressed with his ambition and expertise—he knew how to get a job done.

But Karen had dreams of her own. Raised with three siblings by a single mother, Karen did not have David's resources. She worked three jobs to support herself while finishing an under-graduate degree in chemistry. More than anything, Karen wanted to go to medical school.

David knew about Karen's dream of becoming a doctor. He told her he was proud of her and admired her hard work. She assumed he would be supportive. And he was, until she got down to the nitty-gritty of applying to medical school.

First he was upset because the applications were so expensive. He couldn't understand why she had to apply to eight schools—it was like throwing money out the window. Why couldn't she just try one or two in their area and see what happened?

Then he balked at the idea of moving to another city. He had just started his business and didn't want to start over. While Karen understood this, she also knew that he did 90 percent of his business over the phone or through electronic mail. He could take his business anywhere.

After months of waiting, Karen was accepted into three programs, one of which was only fifty miles from David's office and their home. She breathed a sigh of relief, thinking that fifty miles wouldn't be a problem. If they rented a house halfway between school and David's office, they would each drive only half the distance.

"No way," David said. Maybe she could wait until next year and try to get into the medical school right in town. After all, she was number three on the waiting list; maybe she'd move up. It was Karen's turn to say, "No way."

She enrolled in school, and after the first quarter, she started carpooling with another first-year student named Ken. Already unhappy about the amount of time she was spending away from home, David was further angered by this arrangement. He was not going to let it slide. He started demanding details about her schedule—what time did class start, what time was it over, who was there, whom did she talk with, sit next to, go on break with. He questioned her if she was the slightest bit late, complained that they never had time for each other, and even accused her of having an affair with Ken.

Distraught by David's reactions, Karen asked him to go to marriage counseling. She assured him repeatedly that she was not having an affair, that she loved him and intended to spend the rest of her life with him. But she was worried about him, and about their relationship. His accusations of infidelity were becoming more strident and increasingly offensive. Soon it was not only Ken he suspected, but other students in her study group and one of her professors as well.

David refused to go to counseling, with or without her. He had little time and no respect for mental health professionals. There was nothing they could tell him that he didn't already know. He was disappointed she'd even suggest such a thing. Didn't she think they could handle their own problems? Weary, Karen let it drop for a while. She tried to spend more time with David, and took to studying at home instead of the library.

David felt much more comfortable with Karen around in the evenings. There were times he didn't really think she was having an affair. But other times, he couldn't keep the thought out of his head. He was uncomfortable with the amount of time she was spending with other men and didn't understand how she could be "just friends" with all these guys.

One evening, when the two of them were out having dinner, Karen and David ran into Ken and his girlfriend. The four of them chatted for about ten minutes, and at the end, Karen and Ken arranged to meet for a study session the next day. David could feel himself getting angry. He said nothing until they got to the car.

"I don't understand what you see in him! If you really loved me you wouldn't spend your time studying with him. You know, things were just fine before you started all this medical school business!" He pounded the steering wheel again and again with his fist.

Karen was shaken but remained silent. As mad as he had gotten in the past, she had never seen him hit anything.

The next day when David got home from the office, he found a note on the kitchen table.

Dear David:

I love you very much but can no longer live like this. I thought you would be as proud of me as I was for getting into medical school. I want you to be part of my dream. But we can't go on like this. I would still like us to go to marriage counseling. If you change your mind, you can reach me at Mom's.

Love, Karen

At first he thought she was kidding—a test to see whether or not he'd changed his mind about them getting help. She wouldn't really move out. How could she? She'd never make it. No money. Debt. An old heap for a car.

But her closets were empty.

A familiar feeling crept over him—fear and sadness that grew into anger, then into rage.

"Dammit!" he yelled as he hurled the kitchen chair against the wall. The chair bounced off the table, breaking two glasses.

Still fuming the next morning, David phoned the mental health clinic and spoke with a crisis counselor. "I have to get in right away. Today! My wife left me last night and she says I have to talk to someone before she'll come back."

When David appeared at the clinic a couple of hours later, the psychologist ushered him into his office. After introducing himself he said, "Why don't we start by having you tell me a little bit about why you're here today."

"My wife told me I needed to see someone. She left me, for another guy, I think, but I'm not sure. Anyway, I figured I might as well get in here and get it over with. How long do you think this will take? How many times do I have to come here?"

DEFINING THERAPY

Therapy is the process of treating a problem that gets in the way of effective living.

Far from Hollywood portrayals of exotic encounters with bespectacled therapists who look like descendants of Sigmund Freud, therapy is simply a method of using our resources to solve or manage problems that get in the way of living life comfortably.

There are three basic types of therapy: self-therapy, informal therapy, and formal therapy. No one type of therapy is better than the other, as long as it produces the results we want. Although the majority of this book attempts to demystify formal therapy and its trappings, the other two types are equally important.

Self-Therapy

Anyone who has been to the grocery store knows about self-therapy, because it's impossible to get out of the store without passing the magazine rack. Even if you never cave in to the temptation to thumb through any of the myriad selections, you can still get a feel for the contents by the covers. "Confront Your Fears!" "Ten Ways to Ward Off the Winter Blues," "Three Jim-Dandy Ways to Let Your Boss Know He's a Jerk and Still Get That Promotion!" "What Sex Therapists Won't Tell You: Six Marvelous Methods of Ensuring Orgasm."

Self-therapy is a form of self-care that helps relieve stress and prevent minor irritations from becoming unmanageable. We use self-therapy without even thinking about it. When confused, stressed, or confronted with a dilemma, most of us don't say, "Now I'm going to do therapy on myself." Instead we say things like, "I think I'll go home and take a hot bath," or "I'm going to the gym to shoot buckets," or "Give me some time to think about this."

Effective self-therapy translates well from one situation to the next. For example, when Julie recognized that she was unhappy, she worked to uncover the basis for her dissatisfaction. To do this, she used the same analytical skills that she used in her job. First, Julie identified her problem—she felt unhappy and disinterested in her life. Second, she gathered information about the circumstances that made her feel unhappy (as she would to analyze an unhappy business situation at work, say, a downturn in sales). Third, Julie generated a list of options to improve her situation (just as she would to increase sales). Finally, she reviewed her options and determined the best course of action. Julie's self-therapy, then, involved the same problem-solving process she used at work—clearly identify the problem, target contributing factors, create a list of options, and determine which options would result in a positive outcome.

There are many types of self-therapy, and many problems to which self-therapy may be applied. I once had a client who became anxious every time she had to meet with one of her son's teachers, so she would "rehearse" her part for several days before each meeting. She would put on the outfit she intended to wear, gather her purse and coat, sit on the couch, and envision herself in the classroom with the teacher. The woman prepared a script of what she was going to say and how she would respond to the teacher's questions. She would read the script out loud and practice relaxation techniques she had learned from a book. By preparing herself for each encounter, she was able to follow through with the meetings.

In many cases, self-therapy not only gets us through the minor problems associated with daily living, it helps us survive major catastrophes and devastating circumstances.

In 1982, Ellen Hansen took her two young daughters to their church day care for an evening program. Hansen's oldest daughter, Cassie, asked to go to the bathroom. Hansen followed a couple of minutes later. When she could not locate her daughter, she knew something was wrong. She called the police, then her husband.

Volunteers and police searched all night and part of the next day before finding Cassie Hansen's body in a dumpster not far from the church. She had been abducted and murdered by a local cab driver.

Ellen Hansen's story is a parent's worst nightmare. After alerting the authorities, Hansen went back to the church and prayed. Even today she recalls the feeling of tremendous inner strength from God that kept her from giving up. Over the years it has been this strength, along with the support of friends and family, that has allowed her to go on with her life and have more children.

By turning to spirituality during one of the darkest moments of her life, Hansen engaged in a form of self-therapy. It was a way to take care of herself, garner strength, and overcome her fears. And it worked for her.

We all have the potential to meet our problems head-on. By taking inventory of our resources and continually adding new ones, we become more capable of caring for ourselves. By reading, observing, and experimenting with new perspectives and creative solutions, we improve our chances of surviving life's unpleasant experiences.

Self-therapy has been strongly promoted by hundreds of self-help books over the past several years. Some books are better than others, and some forms of self-therapy are more effective than others. Only you can decide which ones work best for you.

Some of the more common forms of self-therapy include:

- Decision making
- Assertiveness
- Setting goals
- Setting priorities
- Physical exercise
- Prayer
- Massage
- Meditation
- Relaxation techniques
- Journaling

Informal Therapy

Unlike self-therapy, which is an individual endeavor, informal therapy is the process of getting help from those around us: friends, relatives, acquaintances, neighbors, and mentors. Together, these groups of people form networks. Networks are the essence of informal therapy. They are collections of people we have come to rely on for information, opinions, feedback, or support. There are three basic types of networks: social, professional, and familial.

Social networks are made up of groups or individuals we "play" with. These are people with whom we might have dinner, take in a movie, travel, attend a concert, go bowling, have a few beers, or grab a cup of coffee. Members of a social network may also include family members and co-workers.

In an effective network, people are comfortable and easy to talk with or confide in. They offer support in good times and bad. People in our social network let us vent feelings, float ideas, and take risks with the understanding that we will do the same for them.

Professional networks are groups of people we know through work or professional organizations. Some of them are close working associates. Others may be members of the Rotary Club, board members serving the same organization, or colleagues we only see at conferences a couple of times a year. Relationships that grow out of shared hobbies or vocational interests occasionally evolve into social contacts as well.

Family networks can be the toughest of the three. Unlike social and professional networks, we don't usually get to choose our family network. Needless to say, our level of tolerance for family members is much higher than for members of our other two networks. For example, if you've had enough of that bone-headed accountant on your Monday night softball team, you can play on another team or switch to a different night. That's a little harder to do with a boneheaded brother, however. He's family.

Not every member of every network can be counted on to give the same level of support in difficult situations. For example, when her friend Tracy died, Lisa was able to manage those first difficult months by engaging in informal therapy with Tracy's mother, Corrine. Lisa was not only able to grieve, she was able to support Corrine in ways that Tracy's other friends could not. Although their reminiscing was as painful as it was curative, it was a common, welcome vehicle toward healing.

It was much more difficult to talk about Tracy's death with members of her own family or with friends who didn't know Tracy. After the first month, Lisa got the distinct impression that they thought she was taking too much time to get over it. She felt pressured, especially by her parents and siblings, to hurry up and get better. She sensed an impatience that was disappointing and alienating. Her mother wondered aloud why she had to visit Corrine so often and told her to stop going to the cemetery because it was probably only making her more depressed.

Lisa did gain substantial support from new members of her social network—the friends Tracy was with the night she died. By asking questions about what happened, Lisa was able to gather more information about the circumstances of Tracy's death. This was important to Lisa, and somewhat soothing, because there were times when she felt guilty about not being with Tracy when she died. Tracy's friends readily accepted Lisa into their group, which gave Lisa another place she could go to talk about her friend.

Relationships with Informal Therapists

There are several important characteristics of a relationship with an informal therapist. First, the power in the relationship is balanced; one person does not hold power over the other. Informal therapists are network members, very often members of our social network. They are people who will lend their support when we need it, and who will ask for ours in return.

Second, participants give advice freely in an informal therapy relationship. That's partly why these relationships are so helpful. By listening to the opinions of people we care about and respect, we can measure our response against theirs. We ask for advice or feedback in a number of ways—"Can I pick your brain for a few minutes?" "I'd like to bounce something off you if you've got time," or "Let me check this out and see what you think."

A third characteristic of informal therapy is that no money changes hands. The support obtained from an informal therapist is based on the relationship itself. This is important, because as soon as there is an exchange of money, the balance of power shifts, and the relationship is no longer informal.

Finally, informal therapy is reciprocal. This means the role of informal therapist shifts back and forth between friends. Sometimes you give a little help, sometimes you get a little. It is not a conscious changing of the guard, but a fluid movement of time and energy. You know who you can count on, as others know they can count on you.

Formal Therapy

Formal therapy is the process of resolving or managing problems with the help of a trained professional. It is a series of steps a client takes under the guidance of an individual who has been specifically trained to facilitate change. It is not a quick fix. It is not a single answer. It is usually a great deal of hard work.

When David met his therapist for the first time, he expected to get answers that would fix his problem. "How can I get my wife back? Why did she leave in the first place? What should I do now?"

The therapist was slow to answer David's questions; worse yet, sometimes he didn't answer them at all. In fact, the therapist seemed to be asking more questions than he answered. David expected the therapist to act like a consultant, like David did when he was with his own clients. When clients asked questions about what was wrong with their computer system, David gave them an answer—one that would fix the problem, or at least go a long way toward solving it.

By the end of the first session, David was clearly upset. He was disappointed and frustrated because his expectations had not been met, and he wondered if he should continue with therapy. Finally he asked, "So how can you help me? How long is this going to take?"

The therapist explained that his job was not to "fix" David, but to help David find his own answers. David reluctantly agreed to come back for another session.

Formal therapy is similar to informal therapy in that both processes set out to help resolve or manage problems. There are, however, a number of differences between the two.

Relationships with Formal Therapists

One of the most significant differences is that formal therapists are not members of our social network. They are not friends, acquaintances, co-workers, parents, relatives, partners, or neighbors. They have one function and one function only, and they do not cross the line into other aspects of their clients' lives.

The relationship between client and therapist is professional; it is not reciprocal. Healthy client-therapist relationships place a singular emphasis on the emotional and psychological needs of the client, *not the personal needs of the therapist.* This is different from relationships with informal therapists, where support is traded and members look to one another for assistance, comfort, and strength.

Another difference between formal and informal therapists lies in the distribution of power. In informal therapy, both parties have equal power. In formal therapy, the therapist assumes the bulk of the power—as well as the primary responsibility for what happens in the sessions. This does not mean that the therapist is in charge of "fixing" what's wrong. The therapist is simply responsible for ensuring a safe environment so the client can work out his or her problems.

The hallmark of any professional relationship, whether with doctors, lawyers, or business consultants, is the exchange of money. This is true of formal therapy relationships as well. A good therapist is a great listener, but never a friend. An exchange of money indicates the purchase of a service. When clients seek help from a mental health clinician, they agree to purchase what the therapist is selling: expertise, knowledge of human behavior, and problem-solving techniques.

Finally, clients seek help from professionals because they are looking for professional advice. Typically, formal therapists do not hand out the type of advice you might receive from informal therapists. The therapeutic task is to try to decide what is causing the current difficulty, and to help the client resolve it. The therapist's job is not to tell you what to do, nor is it to share with you what he or she would do in your position. It is to help you pinpoint the problem, outline your options, and choose a productive course of action.

CHAPTER TWO

HOW DO I KNOW IF
I NEED THERAPY?

On a desolate stretch of Iowa highway, a lone van peels through the countryside at eighty-plus miles per hour. The roads are good, visibility is clear, and with the sunroof wide open, the van's occupants, two young couples on their way to Chicago, are intoxicated by the smell of freshly mowed fields.

Out of nowhere, a fawn ambles onto the highway and freezes when she sees the approaching vehicle. The young driver swerves to avoid hitting her. He fishtails across the highway and flips the van after hitting a construction barrier. The vehicle lands on its side, trapping the passengers in their seats. Except for blood trickling out the corner of one woman's mouth and the involuntary tremors down the arms and legs of the other, the scene is eerily still.

The first person to come upon the wreckage is a trucker, who uses his radio to call for help. Emergency vehicles scream to the site; workers extricate the victims and rush them off to the hospital. An emergency room physician performs a quick check on each victim before barking out orders for their care.

———

Sam notices that a small mole on the left side of his face is feeling tender. It hasn't changed in size or shape, so he isn't concerned. A couple of weeks later the pain subsides, but the mole seems to be getting bigger. Soon afterward, a physician friend of his says the mole may need professional attention and urges him to see his own doctor.

———

Every winter Larry's knee acts up, the result of an old football injury. It is stiff in the morning but generally loosens when he does the exercises prescribed by a physical therapist. He had been told several times over the years that regular exercise is the best treatment.

Larry doesn't always take the time to follow the therapist's recommendations. Instead, every year just after the weather turns cold, he goes to see the orthopedist, who refers him back to the physical therapist, who gives him a new booklet of exercises. This year is no exception, and Larry is once again told to follow through on the exercise program.

———

All three of these situations describe circumstances requiring medical care or advice. Some situations are life-threatening and need immediate attention. Others are of moderate concern. Still others might be handled through minimal intervention.

The need for mental health treatment runs along this same continuum, ranging from "Help me now!" to "I can do it myself, thanks anyway." At one end are serious conditions that impede our ability to perform our daily routine. In some circumstances, the need for help is so dramatic and so obvious that something must be done immediately.

Other times the need for help is evident but less urgent, like the mole on Sam's neck. If emotional problems do not keep us from our daily routine, we can take the time to assess the situation and decide on a suitable course of action.

Finally, there are times when we are troubled, sad, or upset by ordinary events brought on by the wear and tear of everyday living. These are the psychological equivalent of Larry's knee and can usually be managed without professional intervention, if we exercise common sense.

The decision to seek medical care is commonly based on a change in our physical health. Likewise, the decision to seek mental health care is prompted by a change in our psychological well-being. These changes occur most commonly in our thoughts, feelings, and behaviors. A disturbance in one of these areas can create changes in the other two.

Thoughts, feelings, and behaviors are shaped by a number of forces that fall into one of two categories: internal mechanisms and external events. Before we can solve or manage our problems, we must understand how these forces affect us.

INTERNAL MECHANISMS

Internal mechanisms are personal characteristics that help determine how we respond to the world around us. The most influential mechanisms are biology, personality, and perception. These forces interact with each other, and they help account for the way we think, feel, and act in a variety of situations.

Biology

Researchers have discovered that some psychological characteristics can be passed down from one generation to the next. This means that some individuals may be genetically predisposed to certain mental health conditions.

Take schizophrenia, for example, a devastating disease marked by hallucinations, delusions, and other serious impairments. Medical technology has revealed that the brain structure of people with schizophrenia is quite different from the brain structure of those without it. Furthermore, blood relatives of schizophrenics have a greater chance of developing schizophrenia than other individuals. Both discoveries suggest a biological basis for the disease.

Obsessive-compulsive disorder, a problem characterized by persistent thoughts and ritualistic behaviors, also occurs more commonly among individuals who have an immediate family member suffering from the same problem. The same can be said of depression and anxiety, the two most common complaints among people who seek mental health treatment.

Biology, then, has a profound effect on our thoughts, feelings, and behaviors. If you know you are genetically predisposed toward a mental health condition, you and your therapist will be better prepared to treat symptoms that might develop.

Personality

Personality is the unique combination of qualities that separates one individual from another. Experts have debated for years about which has a greater influence on personality—biology, that which we are born with, or environment, that which we are born into. Although the debate is unlikely to be settled anytime soon, it is clear that both have a significant effect on how we relate to the world.

Research indicates that biology plays an important part in human disposition. Scientists observing newborns in hospital nurseries have shown that babies are born with different temperaments. Some are fussy, others are calm. Some become distressed easily, while others aren't readily bothered.

The temperament a child is born with, however, is only part of the equation. Personality development also depends on a child's environment, and the most influential forces in a child's environment are his or her parents. Some parents are accepting and tolerant, while others become irritated at the slightest disruption. Some are relaxed, others are easily stressed.

Early interactions between a child and his or her parents, combined with the child's own personality traits, will affect the child's ongoing personality development. For example, an anxious child with rigid parents may lack confidence as an adolescent or adult. That same child will have a better chance of becoming self-sufficient and independent with flexible, yet supportive, parents.

Personality characteristics that are established early on are likely to carry over into adolescence and adulthood. For example, kind-hearted and sensitive children are likely to develop into empathic adults. On the other hand, cruel children who are left to their own devices are likely to develop predatory behaviors.

Perception

Perception is the way we view our surroundings and interpret the things that happen to us. It is colored by our past experiences, and it influences the outcome of present and future situations.

Whether we know it or not, our past experiences frequently lead us to make assumptions about the present and the future. For example, the child who grows up in an alcoholic family may learn that his or her needs are not important, promises and commitments are rarely kept, and apologies are worthless because they do not lead to change.

Children who experience physical or sexual abuse, especially at the hands of family members, learn that they will be betrayed by the people they trust. Because these children lack a safety mentor to help them distinguish between safe situations and dangerous ones, they often grow into adults who make poor decisions. This renders them vulnerable to future abuse.

Children who grow up in a stable, loving home learn to trust their environment as well as their own perceptions. As adults, they are better equipped to form satisfying, healthy relationships.

Childhood experiences, combined with our individual personality traits, give rise to our world view—our general perception of the world around us. World views are made up of core beliefs, which guide us in what we do and how we feel. Some core beliefs are healthy and rational. Others are not.

For example, David, the autocratic computer consultant in chapter 1 is unhappy with his wife's decision to go to medical school, and even less enthusiastic about her relationships with male colleagues. Some of David's core beliefs include:

- "I make the major decisions in the relationship for both of us."
- "If I am not in control of the people around me, I won't get what I want."
- "Men and women can never be 'just friends.' "
- "There is something wrong with my wife if she enjoys the company of other men."
- "Anyone who would spend that much time on herself is selfish."

David's core beliefs indicate a need to control the people around him. World views like this are rigid, inflexible, and easily threatened. They are bound to cause problems in David's life.

Biology, perception, and personality are the foundation for how we respond to what goes on around us. Therapy helps us figure out which of these internal mechanisms may be causing us trouble, then generates methods to help us manage the difficulty.

For example, if you develop symptoms of depression for no apparent reason, and you know that both of your parents have been treated for depression, you may be dealing with a biological predisposition for the disorder. This may be treated through medication.

Similarly, if you perceive most individuals as untrustworthy and have a difficult time forming meaningful relationships, a therapist can help you test and change your perceptions that may be contributing to poor social connections. This will improve your "people" judgment and lead to more satisfying relationships.

EXTERNAL EVENTS

External events, like internal mechanisms, can cause disturbances in our thoughts, feelings, and behaviors. If internal mechanisms are the bedrock of how we respond, external events are the "rolling stones" of daily living. External events are situations that occur in our environment. They may be planned or unplanned.

We expect planned events to be less troublesome than unplanned events. Many planned events are joyous occasions that have been long anticipated. Starting a new job, getting married, having a baby, moving to a new town, or retiring are typically positive, planned events. But even well-planned, happy events can throw us off balance, because we're rarely prepared for the changes that accompany them—the prolonged fatigue that comes in caring for a newborn, the initial loneliness upon moving to a different town, the hours of unstructured time that come with retirement. Most major events require a period of adjustment, and this sometimes catches us off guard.

External events are not always planned, however, and chance encounters can radically alter our core beliefs and world view. Some encounters might be considered fortunate, even miraculous. For example, a man who thinks he is unlucky wins the lottery and snatches his home from the jaws of foreclosure. A family beats nearly impossible odds when they find a bone-marrow donor for their son with leukemia.

Many chance encounters are not so uplifting. Some are mere annoyances, for example, a critical remark from a friend or a blunt comment made by a co-worker. Others are unfortunate, like getting fired from a job, missing a promotion, contracting a major illness. Still others are tragic, such as the death of a loved one.

Frequently, it is a collision between our internal mechanisms and external events that prompts us to seek therapy.

"The unbearable lightness of me"

Susan, an attractive sixteen-year-old, is the envy of her friends. She is a straight-A student, captain of the debate team, an ace soccer player, and first-chair flute in the school orchestra. Susan has always been a perfectionist. As a child, she'd burst into tears if she missed a word on her weekly spelling test, and she'd rewrite math assignments instead of hand them in with erasure marks. She was the only one of her siblings who made her bed or organized her closets. Comments on her physical appearance, even positive ones like "You look great today" or "I like your hair" sent her checking anxiously to make sure nothing was out of place.

Susan's parents brought her to a therapist after she had lost an alarming amount of weight. At 5 feet 5 inches tall, Susan weighed 93 pounds—down 32 pounds from her normal weight of 125. She had dropped four clothing sizes in three months, and no longer reached the minimum weight on the growth chart for girls her age. In therapy, Susan spent much of her time explaining how fat she was, how big her stomach was, and how perfect she would feel if only she could lose another ten pounds.

Susan says her obsession with weight started the day her soccer coach gave a lecture on general health. He discussed the need for adequate sleep, productive activity, and nutrition. He told his team to eat foods that were high in fiber and carbohydrates, and pleaded with them to lay off foods with a high fat content. "We don't want any chubby thighs out there, okay girls?" He looked straight to the back of the room where Susan was sitting with two of her friends. Her friends barely noticed the remark, but Susan was horrified. Convinced that the coach was talking about her, she felt ashamed and embarrassed. She decided then and there to lose weight. She went on a starvation diet and started to do exercises targeting her thighs.

Susan's drive for perfection is part of her personality. It allows little margin for error, whether real or perceived. When powerful internal mechanisms like this collide with unpredictable external events, such as the coach's off-the-cuff comment, the results can create drastic changes in an individual's thoughts, feelings, and behaviors.

Susan's Thoughts

- "I'm so fat I'll never be able to wear shorts again."
- "My thighs are huge and ugly."
- "I have to lose at least ten more pounds."

Susan's Feelings

- Embarrassment
- Shame
- Self-disgust

Susan's Behaviors

- Reduced food intake to one small meal a day
- Refused to eat with family at mealtime
- Reluctant to attend social gatherings where food is present
- Angry all the time; highly irritable; lashes out at family members, especially when they tell her she needs to eat
- Started new exercise program—one hour in the morning and two hours after school

"I never promised you a rose garden"

Mark, a business executive in his mid-fifties, had been with a major manufacturing firm for fifteen years. As the vice president of Human Resources, he had shepherded the company through many challenges: diversity training, AIDS in the workplace, the formation of a sexual harassment policy, and changes in worker's compensation regulations, to name a few. The job had changed considerably since he was hired. Back then it seemed the most political decision he'd have to make was whether to send his employees a turkey or a ham for the holidays.

It had been an interesting time in his career, but he was ready for a break. When the company announced a downsizing program that included an attractive early-retirement package, he took it.

Initially, Mark had mixed feelings about leaving corporate life. On the one hand, he would miss the camaraderie he felt with his colleagues and the satisfaction of knowing he'd done a good job. On the other, there would be no more working until midnight on presentations, policies, and reports. And now he could pursue his first love—golf. Mike's wife, Sally, even bought him a new set of Ping golf clubs to celebrate.

But three months into his retirement, the clubs have only made it out of the bag twice. Sally noticed that Mark has become quiet and withdrawn. Instead of calling friends to arrange tee times, he sits in front of the television, flipping through channels with his remote control. Mark sleeps fourteen hours a night, and he's still tired when he gets up in the morning. He has no appetite, and his energy is low. One afternoon, when Sally tried to coax him into going out for a walk, he told her she'd be better off without him.

Although Mark had anticipated a period of adjustment, he was unprepared for the changes that came with retirement. His confidence and self-esteem had largely been artifacts of his job, so when he retired, they diminished. Furthermore, Mark genuinely missed the structure and predictability of his days. He liked knowing that he had to be at work from nine to five, even though his days were frequently hectic and stressful.

Now, its just him and Sally. The days seem long and without purpose. The collision between Mark's personality traits (his competence, his love of problem solving, and his need to be around people) and a planned external event (retirement) produced disturbing changes in his thoughts, feelings, and behaviors.

Mark's Thoughts

- "I am worthless."
- "Nobody needs me."
- "I'd be better off dead."

Mark's Feelings

- Depression
- Despair
- Helplessness

Mark's Behaviors

- Withdrawal from friends
- Decline in activities he previously enjoyed
- Excessive sleep
- Lethargy

MAKING THE DECISION

It can be difficult for individuals to decide if they need help from a mental health professional. We all have problems, but sometimes it's hard to know when those problems are too big to handle on our own.

Fortunately, there are others nearby who can help us make that decision—they'll nudge us in the right direction, and in some cases they'll demand that we get help. In Susan's case, it was her parents. For Mark, it was his wife, Sally.

There are three factors that may motivate us to seek professional help. One is self-examination. Another is observation and feedback from the people around us. Finally, a legal authority may force us into therapy. Often it is a combination of factors that finally pushes us into action.

Self-Examination: "Maybe I should see someone"

Some people are more insightful than others. They have a certain capacity to understand what they do and why they do it. They monitor their actions and reactions on a regular basis, and they make choices designed to help maintain their emotional equilibrium.

People who can recognize changes in their thoughts, feelings, or behaviors are more likely to know when they are in trouble. When they sense they are "off," they will take a corrective action to try to reestablish balance.

Corrective actions compensate for the feeling of having tipped off balance. If you're feeling irritable after a long day at work, you might take a hot bath and settle down with a good book. If you have a fight with your closest friend, you might prefer to exercise for an hour at the gym before calling her to try to work things out. If you're feeling hurt and deceived because you've recently learned that you were adopted, you might consider talking to a therapist. All of these are corrective actions.

While some corrective actions are intuitive, others, like seeking therapy, sometimes require a bit of self-examination. Self-examination means recognizing changes in our well-being, and deciding if we need a professional to help us make these changes.

Julie, the sales rep from chapter 1, recognized that her feelings and behaviors were taking on a negative tone. She had become grumpy and more reclusive. She stopped participating in activities she enjoyed, such as exercising and socializing with friends. Julie considered seeing a therapist, but decided to try to resolve her problems on her own. Since her work environment appeared to be the major culprit, she came up with options that she thought would help her restore balance. If none of her options produced the results she wanted, Julie was committed to getting professional help.

Julie knew she had to do something about the shift in her thoughts, feelings, and behaviors. These changes occurred gradually, leaving little holes in her psychological landscape that made her tired and unhappy. Not all changes are gradual, however. Some blast their way into our lives through a catastrophic event, such as the loss of a loved one. It can be especially difficult for victims of crises to determine if they need therapy. This is when feedback from others can be particularly useful.

Feedback: "Maybe you should see someone"

While it is important to examine ourselves, it is equally important that we listen to and understand the perceptions of those around us, especially those we trust. Friends, relatives, spouses, co-workers, children, and close network members will all let us know how we are doing.

There are two ways to get information from the people around us. One is to take it as it comes. The other is to ask for it.

The information we get from others depends on the rules of each relationship. Honest relationships permit a free exchange of information, even if it is unfavorable. Some relationships do not allow for this. These are governed by unspoken rules like "don't upset the other person" or "don't take risks." In these situations, we receive little unsolicited information, so if we really want to know, we must ask.

Of course, asking a question assumes we are ready and willing to listen to the answer. This is not always easy, especially if the answer is inconsistent with our own perceptions. Let's say David decides to ask his best friend for feedback on the situation between him and his wife. His friend has the gumption to say that David has not been very supportive of Karen's efforts to go to medical school and he can't figure out why he's so jealous. If David is willing to listen to what his friend says, the friend will be honest again in the future, even if David disagrees with him. If David explodes at his friend the way he exploded at Karen, the likelihood of his friend risking an honest response in the future is slim.

When we ask a question, we are obligated to listen to the response—even if we don't like what we hear. If we listen carefully, we will get a view of ourselves from someone else's perspective. And if we hear the same concerns from more than one person, it is a good indicator that we may need outside help.

Getting professional help is usually an individual decision, but there are exceptions.

Legal Authority: "You WILL see someone"

Good decision making is rewarded—we get to keep the privilege. Bad decisions mean that others might step in and make our decisions for us. This is especially true when the decisions we make are dangerous, illegal, or both. For example, if we harm ourselves or others through physical violence, excessive drinking, drug abuse, or gambling, it is likely that legal authorities will take control, at least, temporarily.

We have all heard about prominent people who fell from grace after being arrested for drunk driving, drug possession, stealing, embezzling, or passing bad checks. But these are not just the problems of prominent people. Each of us probably knows or suspects someone who has a problem that is out of control. Sometimes we are that person.

If we are out of control, authorities might refer us to a mental health or chemical dependence professional. For some people, a referral is a much-needed kick in the backside to start making better decisions. For others, referrals are merely an annoyance, nothing more than an effort to force change on the unwilling.

Treatment is hard enough. Conscripting the participant doesn't make it any easier.

AM I READY FOR THERAPY?

Some people are driven to therapy by a need to please a spouse, lover, parent, teacher, or other influential person who encourages them to get help. Nudges from loved ones may be helpful, but when nudges turn into ultimatums, therapy is likely to be hindered by feelings of resentment. Change cannot take place on command.

People who agree to get help in order to please someone else may not be ready for therapy. Timing is essential. When the timing is off, therapy is less likely to succeed.

Timing is a combination of four factors:
- Pain
- A willingness to disclose information
- A commitment to make time for therapy
- Financial resources

Pain

Pain is one of the most important factors in determining when an individual is ready for therapy. There is nothing like pain to motivate change. But pain's effectiveness as an agent for change depends on what we're willing to put up with.

Some people have an enormous tolerance for pain and suffering. They will put up with a staggering (and unhealthy) amount of distress, which can include physical, emotional, psychological, or sexual abuse. People who tolerate the infliction of pain and chaos have a difficult time being assertive. They also have underlying core beliefs that make it hard for them to accept help, such as:
- "I deserve to suffer."
- "No one can help me."
- "There is nothing I can do to help myself."

A good therapist will work to challenge such self-defeating beliefs, but therapists can only do so much. Some beliefs are like hardened steel, unyielding to even the most capable hands. When an individual's beliefs are intractable, it is difficult for change to take place.

While some clients suffer a high tolerance for pain, others live with the opposite problem: no tolerance for pain. Their core beliefs perpetually drive them into a therapist's office:

- "I can't stand this."
- "I don't have to put up with this."
- "Fix it for me."

Many individuals who have no tolerance for pain also have limited coping skills. They may become so dependent on professional help that they find it difficult to function on their own. They occasionally turn into "therapy junkies," craving reassurance, input, and attention not only from mental health professionals, but often from members of the medical establishment as well. A therapist will work with these clients to alter their perceptions and help them believe they are capable of facing life's challenges.

Most people have a middle-of-the-road relationship to pain: some pain is tolerable, but they are ready to ask for help when they reach a certain threshold.

A Willingness to Disclose Information

Many people find it difficult to talk to a stranger. This is especially true when problems are embarrassing, or when they have never been said out loud. Clients sometimes withhold information because they fear the therapist will think they are "crazy." It may take a few sessions for clients to feel comfortable enough to disclose sensitive information.

Other people find it easier to confide in a stranger than in a friend or family member. Strangers know little about us, except what we tell them, and they are less likely to have preconceived notions about who we are.

There's not much that a well-trained mental health professional hasn't heard before, so there's no need to worry about being the "only one like this." Furthermore, everything said during a therapy session is confidential, with the following exceptions:

• In the event of suspected child abuse or neglect, a therapist is legally obligated to report the concern. "Suspected abuse" is a critical concept, because the therapist does not actually determine whether a child has been abused; that's for investigators to decide. (Investigators are usually social workers assigned by a county department, such as Child Protection Services.)

• If a therapist suspects a vulnerable adult is being abused, he or she is obligated to report it to authorities. A vulnerable adult is an adult who is unable to make competent decisions for him- or herself. Vulnerable adults are usually elderly people living with their adult children or in an organized care facility such as a nursing home.

• A therapist must report serious threats made against a specific individual or group. If a therapist is informed of an intent to do bodily harm, he or she will immediately notify the intended victim.

• A client may be taken to the hospital if the therapist suspects that the client is unable to care for him- or herself. This is most common when clients are psychotic, or experiencing auditory or visual hallucinations. Clients who are believed to be dangerous to themselves or others are held for a short time while doctors conduct formal examinations.

A Commitment to Make Time for Therapy

Change takes time. This is a simple presumption, but sometimes we don't take into account the actual amount of time that is required to make a change.

The most obvious time commitment is the time to attend therapy sessions. In other words, clients must be willing and able to make it to scheduled appointments. Many therapists offer evening sessions, but the majority of therapy hours still occur during the day. This means rearranging work schedules, finding baby sitters, and sometimes giving up leisure activities to attend therapy sessions on a regular basis.

Getting to the sessions isn't the biggest commitment, however. It's the time between sessions—when clients do the actual work—which proves to be the most difficult.

Many therapists assign homework to help clients address problems that come up in therapy. For example, clients who want to reduce anxiety may be asked to practice relaxation exercises on a daily basis. Depressive clients may be encouraged to record their thoughts in a journal. Clients who want to be more assertive are often given various assertiveness techniques to practice as opportunities arise.

Therapy often requires clients to learn new behaviors. The most important part of acquiring a new skill is practice, practice, practice. This is as true for individuals learning to play the piano as it is for those learning to reduce stress, lift depression, or assert themselves with their spouse or partner. Without practice, the time, energy, and money we spend on "lessons" are often wasted.

Financial Resources

Mental health care, like other professional help, is not free. Insurance plans sometimes cover all or part of the cost of mental health sessions (see chapter 4). However, whether you have insurance or not, it is important to know how much your treatment costs.

Therapists usually charge by the hour (a therapy hour generally lasts fifty minutes). The cost of a standard fifty-minute session varies by geographic region and the therapist's level of training. In general, clinicians with a doctorate (PhD or PsyD) will charge less than a psychiatrist (MD), but more than a therapist with a master's degree (MA, MSW). Fees for doctorate-level clinicians range from $75 to $140 per hour, social workers charge $60 to $100 per hour, and an hour of psychiatric time usually ranges between $125 and $300.

In addition to the standard appointment, there are several other types of mental health care sessions. The first is known as an "intake," "initial," or "assessment" session. Some intake appointments run longer than the standard fifty minutes, and are charged accordingly. Initial sessions are usually conducted by a nonmedical mental health professional. This individual assesses the nature of the problem and decides whether a psychiatric opinion is necessary. If the therapist believes the client could benefit from medication, the patient is referred to a psychiatrist for consultation.

A "med-check" session is a follow-up appointment to a psychiatric session where medicine was prescribed. During a med-check session, the psychiatrist determines how the patient is doing on the prescribed medication, confirms that the medicine is effective, and monitors any side effects. Med-check sessions usually last fifteen to thirty minutes, so they cost less than a standard fifty-minute session.

Clients who have similar needs are often referred to a third type of session—group therapy. Common problems treated in group therapy include depression, anxiety, eating disorders, passive behavior, and parenting difficulties. Group-therapy sessions usually run longer than an hour (depending on the size of the group, the problem being addressed, and the personalities in attendance). However, the cost of the professional's time can be divided among several clients, so group-therapy sessions are usually less expensive than regular sessions. Standard group rates run between $50 and $90 per person per hour.

A SURVEY

The following questionnaire surveys the three general areas discussed in this chapter: thoughts, feelings, and behaviors. It is intended as an informal tool to bring problem areas into focus and help you decide whether or not to get professional help.

Should I See a Therapist?

Answer the following questions as they apply to your experiences over the past couple of weeks.

	Yes	No
1. I have thoughts that bother me.	___	___
2. It's hard for me to concentrate.	___	___
3. I am having a more difficult time than usual making decisions.	___	___
4. I have the same thoughts over and over again.	___	___
5. I think about hurting or killing myself.*	___	___
6. I think about hurting or killing someone else.*	___	___
7. Others are out to get me.	___	___
8. Things seem hopeless right now.	___	___
9. I feel sad most of the time.	___	___
10. I feel like I'm at my wits' end.	___	___
11. I feel jumpy and nervous.	___	___
12. It seems like I'm always tired.	___	___
13. Life just isn't worth living.*	___	___
14. I am afraid.	___	___
15. I have a hard time sleeping at night.	___	___
16. I am more irritable than usual.	___	___
17. I sleep much more than I used to.	___	___

	Yes	No
18. Others have said they notice a change in me or have mentioned that I'm just not myself.	___	___
19. I often drink or use other drugs to relax or have a good time.	___	___
20. I have some habits that I worry about.	___	___
21. There are times I wonder if I'm normal.	___	___

* If you checked "yes" on any of these, consider seeing a therapist immediately.

Scoring

Because this is not a scientific survey, responses to these questions may only suggest, not predict, a need for help. However, if you answered "yes" to five or more of the questions, please consider calling for an assessment. In general, the more items you checked, the more likely it is that you need help.

CHAPTER THREE

SELECTING A THERAPIST

You've decided to get professional help. Now what? You need to find a suitable therapist, but how? Where do you look and how do you know what to look for? How many different types of therapists and therapies are there? What makes a good therapist? Finding the right therapist might seem confusing at first, but the information in this chapter will help guide you.

First and foremost, therapy is a business, a multimillion dollar industry geared toward helping people feel better and improve their quality of life. It is one of a number of enterprises in which professionals are paid a fee for their information and expertise. In this case, the therapist is the seller and you are the buyer.

When selecting a therapist, think about how you purchase other services. How did you select your physician? Schools for your children? Your auto mechanic, dry cleaner, or dentist? How would you choose a lawyer, accountant, or stockbroker?

Some people spend hours investigating a product or service before signing on the dotted line. They compare prices, explore financing, read consumer reports, and ask friends for recommendations. In other words, they do their homework.

Others are impulse buyers who settle for the first thing that comes along because it looks right, feels good, or was easy to get.

Many are somewhere in-between, picking up information from a variety of sources before making a commitment.

No matter where you fall on this continuum, you're bound to have some questions. The next section explains the different types of therapists and their training, as well as the most common methods used to treat psychological problems.

TYPES OF THERAPISTS

"Psychotherapist" is a generic term loosely applied to anyone who provides mental health services. It is sometimes used by individuals who are in the process of fulfilling their formal training requirements. It is also used by individuals who have been trained in nontraditional programs. A few states now require non-licensed therapists to register with the state Department of Health or a similar organization. Because there is no "psychotherapist" license, people who refer to themselves as such should be questioned about their education and experience.

When choosing a therapist, it is helpful to know something about the educational requirements and training involved in the most common disciplines.

Psychiatrists

All psychiatrists are medical doctors (MD), but not all medical doctors are psychiatrists. In order to attend medical school, students must complete a four-year degree, such as a bachelor of science (BS) or a bachelor of arts (BA). Each medical school has its own set of requirements, but a strong background in science is essential. Competition to get into medical school is fierce, and not everyone who applies gets accepted.

Once admitted, students spend four years studying medicine in both a classroom and clinical setting, after which they receive their MD.

After graduation, students who are interested in becoming a psychiatrist apply for a psychiatric residency. The residency program is either three or four years, depending on the requirements of the university. Once a resident completes the program, he or she is qualified to practice as a general adult psychiatrist. (If a student is interested in becoming a child and adolescent psychiatrist, another year or two of training is required.) After completing their formal training, psychiatrists take a national test known as a board examination, which includes a written portion as well as a test for clinical competency. In addition, psychiatrists must earn a certain number of Continuing Education Credits (CECs) each year to keep their medical license. Credits may be earned by attending workshops, giving presentations, preparing journal articles, or authoring a book, for example.

Psychiatrists assess, diagnose, and treat individuals with mental health problems. Because of their extensive medical training, they are able to review physiological systems (cardiac, endocrine, pulmonary, and so forth) that may influence a patient's health. For instance, some patients who complain of depression are actually suffering from a thyroid problem. Once the thyroid is regulated, the depressive symptoms often disappear.

With the increased emphasis on cost containment in mental health care, there is a trend for psychiatrists to focus on the biological aspects of treatment, which typically involves medication. Psychiatrists are the only mental health providers, with the exception of nurses with a particular kind of advanced training, who can prescribe medication. They monitor the effects of medicines to make sure they are doing what they are supposed to do, and they keep track of any side effects.

In addition to assessment, diagnosis, and medical treatment, some psychiatrists also provide "talk" therapy. They meet with patients on a regular basis to help them resolve their problems.

Rather than conduct ongoing therapy, as they did twenty years ago, most psychiatrists work in conjunction with other mental health professionals to provide the full spectrum of treatment.

Nurses

Most nurses complete a three- to four-year nursing program before earning a bachelor of nursing (BSN). Nurses who work with mental health patients, however, usually have a master's degree as well.

In most states, nurses with a master's degree are known as Clinical Nurse Specialists (CNSs). CNSs have two years of education beyond a bachelor's degree and are trained to treat patients using a more holistic method than their master's-prepared counterparts in psychology or social work.

Most states allow nurses with certain types of advanced training to write prescriptions. This is known as "prescriptive authority," and the requirements to obtain this privilege vary from state to state. Generally, nurses must be trained at the master's level and pass a national examination. They must also have at least 800 hours of clinical experience in advanced practice, as well as 100 hours of work under the guidance of an approved supervisor. There must be a written practice agreement between the nurse and a psychiatric colleague with whom he or she can consult on a regular basis. And finally, nurses must attend and pass classes in psychopharmacology. Even with prescriptive authority, nurses do not have the same type of autonomy as psychiatrists.

Because of their broad education, nurses are also responsible for crisis intervention, patient education, medication management, case management (coordinating all aspects of patient care), physical examinations, and mental status exams.

It is not uncommon for a patient to see a nurse before being referred to a psychiatrist. CNSs rarely work exclusively as therapists; those who do have even more advanced training in psychological processes and methods of therapy.

Psychologists

Psychologists, like psychiatrists and nurses, complete a bachelor's degree before entering advanced training programs. They are educated at either the master's (MA, MS) or doctorate level (PhD, PsyD, or EdD). Some states will only license clinicians for independent practice if they are prepared at the doctorate level.

A psychologist with a master's degree has completed two years of advanced training in both course work and clinical work. Course work addresses areas like personality development, abnormal psychology, tests and measurements, and theories of clinical practice. A field placement in a clinical setting is required during the second year, at which time students see patients (under supervision) and observe seasoned clinicians. Students may work in a hospital, outpatient mental health clinic, school, or any other type of facility that provides the type of work they are interested in.

After graduation, a master's-prepared clinician must practice under an approved supervisor for two years, then take a national licensing examination.

Doctoral students can choose from several types of advanced training programs, not all of which qualify the individual for clinical practice. (Social, Industrial, School, Experimental, Counseling, and Clinical are just a few examples of the advanced psychological degrees available).

All PhD programs emphasize not only subject matter, but research. To earn a PhD, students must complete an original piece of research, then write about it in a formal paper known as a dissertation. A dissertation can take anywhere from two to seven years to complete.

An alternate, and comparatively new, degree for psychology students is the doctor of psychology degree (PsyD). This is also a doctorate, but the emphasis is on clinical work, not research.

After finishing the degree, doctorate level psychologists must complete 2,000 hours of work under a qualified supervisor and pass a national examination before they are licensed to practice independently.

Psychologists perform a number of clinical functions. Like psychiatrists, they assess, diagnose, and treat individuals seeking help. They also conduct formal testing when there is a question of personality, thought, mood, or any other cognitive disorder. Psychologists sometimes work with the legal system to assess offenders and recommend treatment and sentences.

Because psychologists do not have a medical background, they cannot prescribe medications. However, most work with psychiatrists, who can evaluate the need for medicine and offer a second opinion when necessary.

Social Workers

Social workers who provide psychotherapy generally have a master's degree. Some continue on for a doctorate in social work (DSW), especially if they are interested in teaching at the college or university level.

Individuals who seek a master's in social work (MSW) come from a variety of backgrounds. Some have a BA in social work, but many start with a degree in a different field, such as psychology, education, or nursing. Most advanced social work programs take two years and include both course work and clinical work. The two main areas of concentration are direct practice (clinical work) and human services management (administration).

Those wanting to work as clinical social workers take the direct practice concentration and study methods of assessment and therapy. Philosophies vary from school to school, but many social work programs stress an "ecological" or "systems" model of intervention. This model focuses on the individual in his or her environment: family, school, work, church, and community settings. It also attends to larger social issues, such as ethnicity and gender. This is somewhat different from traditional training in psychology, where the emphasis tends to be primarily on the individual, with comparatively little attention paid to broader environmental issues.

Clinical social workers who provide direct therapy are usually licensed at the level of Licensed Independent Clinical Social Worker (LICSW). To earn this license, social workers must complete their degree, meet all field placement requirements, practice for 2,000 hours under a qualified supervisor, and pass a national examination.

Marriage and Family Therapists

Like other mental health clinicians, Marriage and Family therapists hold advanced degrees. Whereas other clinicians study under only one university department, Marriage and Family therapists may choose more than one, including Social Work, Psychology, Family Social Science, Child Development, or Psychiatry.

Marriage and Family therapy has been recognized as a specialty area since the mid-1950s, but therapists have only been licensed since the late-1980s. To qualify for this license, a clinician must complete course work in human development, family systems, theory, assessment, treatment, and ethics. Furthermore, the student is required to practice for 1,000 hours under the supervision of an approved Marriage and Family therapist, then pass a national licensing exam.

If you are seeking therapy for a marital or family problem, be sure to select a therapist who is specifically trained to deal with these issues.

A Word About the Clergy

When troubled, many people turn to the clergy for help. This is appropriate when the trouble involves spiritual or religious concerns. But when life becomes unmanageable because of an unhealthy response to stress, trauma, or crisis, get thee to a well-trained therapist!

Some members of the clergy are qualified mental health professionals, but these are few and far between. Most are not trained to treat mental disorders. They will be unable to help you, and there is a good possibility they will make the situation worse through well-intended, but bad, advice. A competent spiritual adviser will refer you to a bona fide mental health professional when the situation requires it.

If you choose to see a member of the clergy, ask carefully about training and credentials. Therapists are supposed to have their diplomas and licenses hanging on the office wall. Read them.

TYPES OF THERAPIES

Over the past thirty years, the number of different therapies has grown exponentially. There were roughly sixty different major forms of therapy in the 1960s.[1] By the 1980s, this number had reached over four hundred.[2] Needless to say, it would be impossible to review all forms of therapy here. The purpose of this section is to provide a brief overview of the most common therapies available.[3]

Psychoanalysis / Psychodynamic Therapy

Psychoanalysis, or psychodynamic therapy, is the oldest form of individual therapy. It is based on the clinical work of Sigmund Freud, a physician who emphasized the interpersonal causes and treatment of mental illness.

Although psychoanalysis acknowledges biological factors, it places an emphasis on internal conflict—sex and aggression, personal and societal standards, and childhood trauma (abuse, neglect, loss, and abandonment). In order for psychoanalysis to be effective, patients must be able to describe and interpret their symptoms in interpersonal terms. For example, "I get depressed when my wife ignores me," or "I become anxious in relationships because I fear getting rejected."

Psychoanalysis traditionally requires a long course of treatment, often several sessions per week. In psychoanalysis, the therapist gathers information by encouraging the patient to discuss whatever comes to mind. This is called free association, which Freud likened to sitting in a train and describing whatever passes by the mind's window.

The way patients interact with their therapist is similar to the way they interacted with important figures from their childhood. The reenactment of these earlier relationships is called transference.

In psychodynamic therapy, patients who are hesitant or unable to discuss their problems are adhering to familiar, but maladaptive, behavior. This is called resistance.

Psychoanalysis is nondirective, meaning that the patient who asks a direct question is unlikely to get a direct answer. Except in cases where patients are suicidal or homicidal, the psychodynamic therapist will generally refrain from giving advice. The therapist's role is to listen, and to help patients develop healthier ways of relating to themselves and others.

Person-Centered Therapy

Person-Centered therapy, formerly known as Client-Centered therapy, was developed in the 1940s by Carl Rogers. Unlike psychoanalysis, where the therapist is cast in the role of expert, Person-Centered therapy views the client as his or her own expert. In other words, clients have the ability to understand themselves and to change unhealthy thoughts, feelings, and behaviors into healthy ones. The therapist's job is to create an optimal therapeutic environment to help these changes take place.

The Person-Centered therapist demonstrates genuineness, empathy, and unconditional positive regard for the patient. This is in direct contrast to the professional distance of the psychoanalyst.

"Genuineness" is a willingness to relate to the client on a more personal level. "Empathy" means the therapist can appreciate the client's experiences. "Unconditional positive regard" refers to the therapist's ability to accept the client's decisions, thoughts, and feelings without judgment. These three characteristics lead to a healthy therapeutic relationship and an increase in the client's self-esteem. Both are essential for therapy to be successful.

Like psychodynamic therapy, Person-Centered therapy is considered nondirective. This may be frustrating to clients who expect advice or feedback from their therapist. Person-Centered therapists do not give advice, nor do they directly challenge the client's experience.

The length of treatment in Person-Centered therapy varies based on the needs of the client.

Cognitive Behavioral Therapy

Cognitive Behavioral Therapy (CBT) grew out of work conducted by Aaron Beck at the University of Pennsylvania in the 1960s. The basic premise of CBT is that our thoughts play a significant role in determining our feelings and behavior. Mental health problems arise when we perceive, interpret, or act on information in dysfunctional ways, meaning ways that impede our ability to carry on from day to day.

Take, for example, the young man who becomes upset when his live-in girlfriend goes out with her friends instead of staying home with him to watch football on TV. He tells himself that she doesn't love him. He feels abused by her and thinks about asking her to move out. Then he becomes depressed at the prospect of life without her. Because he misinterprets his girlfriend's actions, the young man responds to his situation in a dysfunctional manner.

The goal of CBT is to help clients test their perceptions for accuracy and change dysfunctional perceptions into more helpful ones.

Unlike psychoanalytic and Person-Centered therapies, Cognitive Behavioral Therapy is directive and highly structured. The patient and therapist work together to determine the treatment goals, and the therapist assigns homework in between sessions to help the patient develop new ways of thinking, acting, and feeling. CBT typically lasts between eight and twenty sessions.

Marriage and Family Therapy

Marriage and Family therapists believe that troubled families are the result of unhealthy patterns of interaction. This might involve problems with communication, family roles, or the family's relationship with the community. As a result of this "systems" view, the therapist will often ask the entire family to attend therapy sessions, so the therapist can observe the complete system before making recommendations.

A family needs to maintain its balance in order to operate smoothly from day to day. This balance is known as "homeostasis." When a crisis occurs, a family may be thrown off balance. The goal of the Marriage and Family therapist is to help the family return to a healthy state of homeostasis.

Like the Cognitive Behavioral therapist, the Marriage and Family therapist plays an active role in therapy, serving as a guide to help facilitate change. He or she may assign homework to help members practice the changes they need to make.

Eclecticism

One of the major trends in therapy is the tendency for therapists to use techniques from a number of different schools of thought. The eclectic therapist chooses his or her methods of therapy from a broad, but well-defined, base. The main point of eclecticism is to fit the method of therapy to the client, rather than force the client into a method of therapy that may not be a good fit.

The Brief Therapies

Brief therapy is simply a term applied to any therapy of limited duration—usually twenty sessions or less. All of the therapies discussed in this chapter may be practiced as brief therapy by clinicians who have been trained to do so. Brief therapy is also called "solution-focused," "problem-oriented," or "time-limited" therapy.

Despite their different theoretical bases, all brief therapies have the following characteristics:[4]

• Treatment usually lasts twenty sessions or less.

• Therapists ask specific, goal-directed questions (instead of the open-ended questions familiar to long-term therapists).

• Therapists assess patients rapidly, usually within the first three sessions.

• Therapists help patients identify specific behavioral goals for treatment (instead of focusing on changes in personality).

• Therapists actively guide and direct patients toward change.

• Patients terminate treatment once their goals are met (although they are invited to return for future treatment if the need arises).

• The relationship between patient and therapist is established quickly (this could take months in long-term treatment).

• Therapists are flexible and can draw from a number of theories and techniques to help patients reach their treatment goals.

It's Your Choice

Most people don't set out to find a good social worker or a good psychologist—they're simply looking for a good therapist. Theoretically, any clinician could conduct any type of therapy (except prescribe medication), as long as they have been adequately trained and supervised. To find out about a therapist's training, either ask the therapist directly, or call the appropriate licensing board to request a list of "competencies," or treatments and conditions that the therapist is licensed to practice.

Clients rarely ask questions of their therapists. Too often they make assumptions about professionals in general: "They must be good or they wouldn't be here," "They don't want to answer my questions," or "They will think badly of me if I ask."

Remember, you are the consumer. As the consumer, you have the right to ask questions about education and training, clinic policies, and any other information that will affect the care you receive.

One Therapist at a Time

In general, behavioral health care should only be provided by one therapist at a time. There are a number of reasons for this. First, therapy is a complicated process, and different therapists have different approaches to the same problem. Seeing more than one therapist creates confusion for the patient, because what one therapist might emphasize may seem irrelevant to another.

Second, having more than one therapist gives patients an excuse for not changing their problematic behavior. It is too easy to get stuck in a pattern of "Well, my other therapist says . . ." which distracts people from making the changes they want and need to make. Seeing more than one therapist on an ongoing basis is like having too many cooks in the kitchen—it gets hot, crowded, and uncomfortable.

Third, therapy is expensive. Even if insurance pays for treatment, getting help from more than one therapist at a time is redundant, expensive, and an inefficient use of resources.

Finally, therapy is time consuming. It can be difficult to arrange an already busy schedule to accommodate another hour or so of therapy every week.

Bearing all this in mind, there are some exceptions to the only-one-therapist-at-a-time rule.

• The primary therapist sees a potential need for medication and refers you to a psychiatrist.

• You participate in family therapy to deal with troublesome family issues, but you remain in individual therapy to work on individual issues.

• Your therapist recommends that you attend group and individual therapy at the same time, so the treatments augment each other (for an eating disorder and post-traumatic stress disorder, for example).

• Your therapist refers you to a psychologist for testing.

• The therapist seeks a second opinion or a consultation about your diagnosis.

WHAT MAKES A GOOD THERAPIST?

Some mental health professionals are better than others. This is true of any industry. To distinguish a good therapist from a bad one, keep in mind that a good therapist:

- Understands you
- Is respectful
- Is empathic
- Has been well trained
- Only treats those conditions he or she is trained to treat
- Helps you make changes *you* want to make (not only changes the therapist thinks you should make)

For example, if you want to learn how to communicate with your husband, but your therapist insists that you talk about your early childhood, you may end up a dissatisfied consumer. If you are having trouble getting along with your fifteen-year-old, but your therapist repeatedly directs you to discuss your sex life, something is wrong. If you feel guilty for having recently placed your mother in a nursing home, and your therapist never really lets you talk about that, you will not get what you need.

It's fine to discuss other issues in therapy, but there should be a connection between the therapist's direction and your own goals.

Researchers have spent years trying to determine what traits in a therapist are most likely to result in positive change in clients. They have looked at some of the most common traits: age; gender; socioeconomic status; ethnicity; personality; emotional well-being; and beliefs, values, and attitudes.

In general they have found the following:[5]

• The age of the therapist is not especially important. Clients do as well with older therapists as they do with younger ones.

• A therapist's gender does not appear to make a difference for either male or female clients.

• Clients do better when their therapists are well adjusted, emotionally healthy, and have high self-esteem.

• Clients get worse when they are working with therapists who are distressed or disturbed.

• Most therapists do not consider religious themes to be within the scope of psychotherapy.

• Female clients fare better with therapists who hold nontraditional views of women than with those having highly traditional ideas about women's roles.

• In general, therapists are more accepting than members of the general public when it comes to sexual expression, personal autonomy, and assertiveness. They tend to encourage assertiveness and are less tolerant of submissive behaviors.

• Minorities are less likely than whites to seek out traditional mental health services.

• Drop-out rates are higher among minority clients with white therapists than among clients who share the same ethnic background with their therapist.

• There are significantly fewer therapists from minority groups than there are from the majority culture.

WHERE TO LOOK FOR A THERAPIST

Looking for a therapist is much easier when you know where to start. The following sources may be helpful.

The Insurance or Managed Care Company

All insurance companies publish their policy benefits, including what they cover and what they don't. This information is usually compiled in a booklet, sometimes called a benefits handbook or certificate of coverage. This handbook tells you which treatments are covered and which therapists will be reimbursed for their services.

Many policies will pay for therapy with a psychiatrist or doctorate-level clinician, but will not pay for a therapist trained at the master's level. Others may pay for visits with a doctorate- or master's-prepared clinician, but only if the provider belongs to the insurance plan's network. (A network is a group of providers who have been pre-approved by the insurance plan to deliver mental health services at a negotiated rate.) While your plan may allow you to choose someone outside of the network, it may not pay as much of the bill.

If you intend to use your insurance to pay for treatment, be sure you understand the guidelines and follow them. Ignoring those guidelines could cost you more money in the end. Insurance companies will either deny payment outright, indicating that treatment was not pre-authorized or pre-certified, or pay at a reduced, penalized rate.

Community-Based Resources

If you have no insurance, or if your policy excludes treatment for mental health care, you will be responsible for payment. Do not let this stop you from getting help! There are a number of nonprofit agencies that provide low-cost mental health treatment for individuals with limited or no coverage. Because many of these organizations are facing financial cutbacks, some have started accepting, and in some cases actively seeking out, third-party payment (insurance reimbursement). Also, with the high demand for low-cost or free services, the waiting list could be long.

Organizations providing low-cost mental health treatment include community mental health clinics; family services agencies; Jewish family services; community services for gays and lesbians; and other agencies funded by foundations, grants, and private donations.

For a list of community-based services, check your phone book or call information. You can also check with a family physician, nurse triage phone line, after-hours medical clinic, or mental health clinic.

Employee Assistance Programs

Many companies hire mental health providers to work in their Employee Assistance Program (EAP). An EAP counselor is typically a master's-prepared therapist who sees individuals for short-term counseling. Treatment usually lasts no more than six sessions. (The employer, who pays for the treatment, determines the limit on the number of sessions allowed.) If more treatment is necessary, the EAP counselor will refer the patient to a provider on his or her insurance plan.

In some companies, EAP therapy takes place at work. This can be an advantage, since patients don't have to take as much time off work to see a therapist. Some employees, however, are uncomfortable going into a therapist's office located at their workplace.

Employees can often see an EAP counselor without notifying their employer. However, if your supervisor refers you to an EAP provider for work-related issues, you may be asked to sign a release of information form. This allows the therapist to talk with your supervisor about his or her clinical impressions, diagnosis, and treatment recommendations.

Professional Associations

Many therapists belong to professional associations, such as a state Psychological Association, Association for Marriage and Family Therapy, and Psychiatric Association. These organizations are listed in the phone book. Many maintain lists of professionals and their areas of expertise, which can help you identify therapists in your neighborhood. These are known as referral lists and are updated annually. Referrals are free to anyone looking for a mental health clinician. (Professionals are usually charged a small fee to be listed in the referral directory.)

Professional associations are sometimes confused with professional boards. Professional mental health boards regulate service providers; protect the public; and deal with matters of licensure, behavior, and discipline.

Professional associations, on the other hand, offer educational opportunities for members and sponsor annual meetings and awards. In addition, they lobby certain state and federal legislation, promote their field of discipline to the public (such as psychology or social work), and serve as a resource to the media.

Friends

Friends can be an excellent resource, especially if you feel comfortable talking to them about your problems. There's a good chance that at least one of your friends has been in therapy at some point. This person might be willing to give you the name of his or her therapist. If you have never been in therapy before, see if your friend is willing to discuss his or her experience with the process. This can be especially helpful if you're feeling apprehensive about getting professional help.

Phone Directory

Mental health clinicians can also be found in the Yellow Pages. Listings are usually by profession, such as "psychologists," "psychiatrists," or "family therapists." Some books will simply list "psychotherapists." Although the Yellow Pages does not give specific information about providers, it's a handy way to gather the names of professionals in your neighborhood.

GETTING IN

Now that you have an idea of what you're looking for and where to find it, there are a few other factors to consider: urgency, accessibility, and cost.

Urgency

Mental health professionals generally recognize three levels of urgency:

Non-urgent: "Another couple of weeks isn't going to make much difference. I'll take the first available appointment."

Semi-urgent: "I need to talk to someone soon."

Urgent: "I have to see someone NOW!"

The more urgent the request, the less control you have over who you will see—for that day, anyway. Most outpatient mental health clinics have some capacity to handle crisis situations in person and over the phone, but it's limited. Call ahead to let the clinic know you are coming in so they can arrange for someone to see you. It's easier to get in for a crisis appointment at a specific clinic if you have already been seen by a therapist there. If you have never been seen at that facility, staff may encourage you to call a different clinic—one that is better equipped to see you immediately and on an ongoing basis.

County crisis centers also provide crisis intervention. In situations that are dangerous or life-threatening—for example, if you feel like you're going to hurt yourself or someone else—go to a hospital emergency room, where medical staff can evaluate you.

Semi-urgent and non-urgent appointments should be made at the outpatient mental health clinic where you intend to receive ongoing care. When you call for your first appointment, be honest about your needs. If you must see someone immediately, say so. Staff who schedule appointments are not mind readers, so this is no time to be shy.

Accessibility

One of the hottest issues in mental health care today is accessibility—making sure the services you need are available when you need them. This can be tricky from the clinic's perspective. Clinic managers need to keep therapists busy enough to generate sufficient revenue, but they must also leave enough time for the occasional crisis client, phone call, consultation, or report.

Accessibility is generally referred to as a quality of care issue. You may have signed up with the most brilliant, effective, and competent therapist who ever sat in a chair. But if his or her schedule is so booked up that you can only get appointments once every two months, and you need to be seen once every two weeks, then you are getting substandard care. If your needs cannot be met within an acceptable time frame, look for a different therapist.

Cost

There are two ways to pay for therapy: either you pay, or your insurance company pays.

If you have health insurance, check to see if it covers mental health treatment. If it does, decide whether or not you want to use it. Some people choose not to use their insurance because they are concerned about being "discovered." This, unfortunately, stems from the archaic notion that anyone who needs to see a therapist is "crazy." Rather than risk being found out, some individuals choose to pay for treatment on their own.

The other rationale for not using insurance is the usually unfounded fear that getting help will have a damaging effect on future employment.

Occasionally, people choose not to use their insurance because they don't want to hassle with the insurance company. Unfortunately, some therapists are all too willing to feed this mind-set, particularly if a client is covered by a managed care company. Don't let this happen. Watch for comments like these:

- "You only have ten sessions, so I'm afraid we won't be able to do very much."
- "Your insurance company is running your treatment—it doesn't matter what I say."
- "I can't believe what they make us do nowadays just to be able to see our clients!"

There is nothing wrong with a therapist advocating for his or her client. A good therapist might say, "Your insurance company has authorized ten sessions to start with. Let's see how far we get with those, and if we need more, I can talk with them and see what we can do."

A therapist should never air his or her dislike of insurance guidelines in front of you. It is unprofessional, and unnecessary. Furthermore, such antagonism interferes with effective treatment. If you think your therapist is setting you up to fight with your insurance company, consider finding a new therapist.

You will have to pay for therapy yourself if *(a)* you do not have insurance, *(b)* you decide not to use your insurance, or *(c)* your policy excludes treatment for mental health. A word of caution: Price does not always reflect quality. A therapist charging $175 an hour and making $150,000 a year is not necessarily better than the therapist making $45,000 a year working for a managed care clinic or nonprofit organization. As in other businesses, the cost of therapy is often related to overhead, demand, the financial aspirations of the business owner, and what the market will bear.

Before committing to a therapist, understand what your costs will be. Ask about a payment plan and whether there's a penalty for late payments. Even the best insurance plans have co-payments, so know what kind of financial commitment you are making.

A Final Note

When selecting a therapist, choose someone you are comfortable with, someone you feel you can trust. After your first few sessions, evaluate your decision. Are you getting what you had hoped for? Is the therapist tracking your needs? Do you agree on goals? If there is homework, does it seem reasonable? Does the therapist's style of therapy fit with your personality? Does the therapist's personality fit yours?

If you are not satisfied with the therapist and the therapy process, talk to your therapist about your concerns. If you are still uncomfortable, ask to be transferred to another therapist, or let the therapist know you will be looking for someone else.

Not every therapist can treat every patient. Therapy is a partnership, and the outcome is only satisfying if you're working with someone who can help you fix the problems you think need fixing.

NOTES

1. Raymond Corsini and Danny Wedding, eds., *Current Psychotherapies, Fifth Edition,* (Itasca, Illinois: Peacock, 1995), 10.

2. Sol Garfield and Allen Bergin, *Handbook of Psychotherapy and Behavior Change,* (New York: John Wiley & Sons, 1995), 6.

3. If you are interested in a more in-depth explanation of the different therapies available, you might want to pick up a copy of *Current Psychotherapies, Fifth Edition,* (Itasca, Illinois: Peacock, 1995), edited by Raymond Corsini and Danny Wedding. Although this is a textbook for students starting out in clinical training programs, it is easy to read, well written, and provides detailed information about the fifteen most common therapies used today.

4. Simon H. Budman, *Forms of Brief Therapy,* (New York: Guilford Press, 1981), 461.

5. The information regarding therapist characteristics is a summary of findings from "Therapist Variables," a chapter written by Larry E. Buetler, Paulo P. Machado, and Susan Allstetter Neufeldt for a book entitled *Handbook of Psychotherapy and Behavior Change,* edited by Sol Garfield and Allen Bergin, (New York: John Wiley & Sons, 1995).

CHAPTER FOUR

INSURANCE AND MANAGED CARE

It's been a rough couple of years and you haven't had a real vacation in you-don't-know-how-long. After the usual excuses about timing, money, the kids, and the amount of work you have to do, you throw up your hands, say "the heck with it," and decide to take a trip.

After much deliberation about where to go and how to get there, you settle on a cruise. You've never been on a cruise before, but the idea came highly recommended by several friends who are more than willing to ply you with tantalizing information. You take notes on cruise lines, destinations, and costs. You contact a local travel agent who provides you with an alluring array of travel brochures. You finally decide where you want to go and how much you want to spend. The agent gladly puts together an itinerary, carefully explaining what is covered in the package price and what is not. Satisfied that you are getting a reasonably good deal, you sign on the dotted line.

Now imagine the same scenario again—enthusiastic friends, a pleasant travel agent, wonderful brochures, but no price. Would you still sign on the dotted line?

Let's hope not.

Making a responsible purchase requires an understanding of the financial obligation that goes along with it, whether you are purchasing a cruise, a car, a college education, or therapy.

You wouldn't think about buying a car without knowing the price, or registering for a class without checking the tuition. Yet, everyday, people sign up for therapy without knowing what it costs or how it will be paid for. Many people assume insurance will cover it, but they don't know what "it" is. In no other industry are we such cavalier consumers.

The first three chapters of this book describe the preliminary aspects of therapy: defining it, weighing the decision to buy it, and learning about different types of therapies and therapists.

Before moving directly into a discussion about the actual process of therapy, we will spend some time exploring the business side of the industry. Understanding the mental health benefits of your insurance policy is crucial to receiving high-quality care. Your benefits will determine what kind of therapy your insurance will pay for, which providers you can select, and what your financial obligations will be.

The purpose of this chapter is to acquaint you with the economics of therapy. It discusses your financial responsibilities, as well as your insurance company's, and it introduces you to the concept of managed care. This basic information will go a long way toward eliminating unpleasant surprises.

As I mentioned in the last chapter, there are two ways to pay for therapy: you pay, or your insurance company pays.

Understanding payment requires a basic knowledge of how insurance plans are structured. You may be tempted to skip over this chapter. Don't. Take a few minutes to review the information. The goal here is to help you become a more savvy consumer of mental health services, not to turn you into an insurance guru. Besides, it's not nearly as painful as it sounds.

INSURANCE

There are two main categories of health care insurance: public and private.

Public insurance plans are those that are designed, purchased, and paid for by the government with tax dollars. Recipients are individuals in certain well-defined groups. The elderly may receive Medicare, for example, and low-income women with children are eligible for Aid to Families with Dependent Children (AFDC).

Private health insurance is purchased by either a business (for employees and their family members) or an individual.

When individuals buy health insurance on their own, they are usually self-employed or working for a company that does not provide health care coverage.

In order to qualify for an individual health care policy, applicants must go through an underwriting process, where the insurance company assesses the risk of the applicant(s) and decides whether or not to issue the policy. Not everyone who applies for insurance will get coverage. If you or a member of your family suffer from an ongoing medical or psychiatric illness, called a pre-existing condition, the insurance company may: *(a)* refuse to issue the policy, *(b)* issue the policy but refuse to cover any pre-existing conditions, or *(c)* cover treatment for pre-existing conditions but charge a higher rate. Knowing this, you may be tempted to withhold information about your health status when applying for insurance. Don't. If the insurance company discovers that you have falsified information, it can cancel your entire policy.

Buying insurance on your own is expensive, sometimes prohibitively so. Even if you qualify, the monthly price tag may be more than you can afford to pay. That's why many people take advantage of health care coverage offered by employers.

There are significant advantages to getting insurance through work. Most notably, the cost is lower. Often, and especially with larger companies, employers will pay a significant portion—sometimes all—of your health care premium (the amount you or your employer must pay for your health care coverage). This could represent a significant savings—sometimes several hundred dollars per month depending on your plan, the portion paid by your employer, and the number of family members to be insured. Employers usually get a group discount, so even if your employer contributes nothing to the monthly premium, your cost will be less than if you were to buy insurance on your own.

Some employers buy health care plans that guarantee coverage of anyone who wants to join. This can be a tremendous advantage if you or a member of your family has a pre-existing condition. Plans like these allow you to buy health insurance when you otherwise might not qualify for it.

Insurance companies set different premiums for different employer groups. They base their rates on either community ratings or experience ratings.

Community ratings have been used by a number of Health Maintenance Organizations (HMOs), which charge the same rate for members in similar age and gender categories, regardless of the overall health of the employer group.

Experience ratings track the amount of medical and mental health dollars spent by each employer group in a given amount of time, usually twelve to twenty-four months. Groups with younger, healthier, and more active employees pay lower rates than groups with an aging or less healthy population. Employer groups who use a great deal of medical and mental health care end up with higher monthly rates than those with a healthier work force. That is why many employers stress health and fitness for their employees. Healthy employees use fewer health care resources, which keeps annual premiums low.

Not every insurance policy covers treatment for behavioral health problems. An employer's decision to include it in a policy is based on two factors: legal requirements and his or her attitude toward behavioral health care.

Some states require all health care policies to include a certain amount of coverage for behavioral health treatment, but mandated benefits like these are marginal. Other states have parity laws, which require equal coverage for both behavioral health and medical problems.

Still other states have no minimum requirements, so employers may limit behavioral health care coverage, or omit it altogether. In states that have the minimum requirements, employers will provide basic coverage or offer more than the minimum requirement. It depends on the employer's attitude toward behavioral health care.

Over the past several years, it has become expensive for employers to provide health care coverage for their employees. For example, Donna Martin runs a small manufacturing plant that employees 100 people. Nearly all of them have families. Ten years ago she could buy a good insurance plan for $210 per month per family. Back then she paid the entire amount for each employee, so the monthly cost to her business was $21,000. Today that same plan for those same 100 people costs her $390 per month, per family. Now her total monthly cost is $39,000. In order to stay competitive, she has to pass along some of that cost to her employees, whose share of the premium has gone from nothing to $200 per month. Donna is unhappy because she isn't able to provide for her employees as she has in the past. Her employees aren't happy, either, because their annual cost-of-living increases are being eaten up by the ever-increasing costs of health care.

Buying health care coverage for yourself or your business is an expensive venture. When employers purchase a health care package, they can choose from one of three different plans—an indemnity plan, a self-insured plan, or a managed care plan.

Indemnity Plans

Indemnity plans are plans that indemnify, or pay back, some of what you have spent on health care, minus your deductible and your co-payments.

The deductible is the amount of money you must spend on health care every year—out of your own pocket—before insurance takes over paying the bills. (Deductibles usually range from $250 to $2,000 or more, depending on how the plan is written.) For example, if your deductible is $500, you must pay the first $500 of your health care costs before insurance will pay anything. If you spend nothing until December and then get sick, you will not be reimbursed for the first $500 you spend at the doctor's. If you are still sick in January and need to see a doctor again, you will have to pay the $500 all over again before your insurance takes over.

Your co-payment is the part of the bill that you must pay even after you have met your deductible. This is a fixed percentage or dollar amount, such as $30 for every office visit, or $60 for every visit to the emergency room. Many insurance plans are known as 80-20 plans, which means that for most charges, the insurance company pays 80 percent and you pay 20 percent. Others insurance plans have different splits: 70-30 or 90-10, for example.

In indemnity plans, behavioral health benefits are usually separate from medical benefits, and the benefit levels are not necessarily identical. For example, your plan may allow you to spend up to 365 days in the hospital for a medical problem, but only 30 days per year for a mental health problem. In some plans, it is not unusual for mental health co-payments to run as high as 50 percent—you pay half and the insurance company pays half—and only up to a certain dollar amount. Let's say your plan pays 50 percent for outpatient visits, up to a maximum of $35 per session. Your therapist's fee is $100, which means you must either pay $65 per session, or try to negotiate a lower fee with the therapist. In addition, your plan will only pay a maximum of $10,000 per calendar year and $30,000 over a lifetime. With the typical inpatient psychiatric bed costing roughly $1,000 per day, it would be easy to exhaust a benefit package like this in no time at all.

Indemnity plans are the most expensive health care plans on the market today. Between 1993 and 1996, rates for indemnity plans increased 29 percent. Not surprisingly, employers are choosing these plans less and less frequently. In 1996, the average cost to enroll an employee in an indemnity plan was $3,739. Of all employees enrolled in health care plans nationwide, only 23 percent belong to an indemnity plan.[1]

Self-Insured Plans

Rather than purchase coverage through an insurance company, some employers opt for a self-insured plan. With this plan, an employer sets aside a pool of money to pay for future health care costs. There are no premiums. The employer chooses which services are covered under the plan, but he or she usually hires a company to monitor coverage and administer claims.

To determine the size of the fund, the employer reviews his or her health care costs from the previous year. Employers may also purchase a re-insurance product—a second type of insurance that pays the difference when *(a)* a single claim exceeds a predetermined dollar amount, or *(b)* the group's total expenses exceed a predetermined dollar amount.

Let's say that Donna Martin decides to self-insure. She sets aside a certain amount of money to cover her employees' projected health care costs for one year. She also buys a re-insurance product that will take over payments if any one claim exceeds $150,000, or if her employees use more than $300,000.

One of Donna's employees has a baby in her seventh week of pregnancy. The baby is very ill and requires $200,000 worth of medical care before it leaves the hospital. Donna's self-insurance fund will pay the first $150,000, then her re-insurance will take over and pay the additional $50,000. This way, Donna will not go bankrupt.

Self-insured plans can be advantageous to both employer and employee. The plan may be less expensive than plans purchased through an insurance company, and benefits can be tailored to meet the needs of the employees. But self-insured plans are not usually subject to the same governmental regulations that apply to other insurance plans, which means they do not have to provide minimum benefits.

MANAGED CARE—WHAT IS IT?

The term "managed care" is used to describe health care plans that strive to deliver service in a clinically effective, cost-efficient manner. The goal of managed care is to provide an adequate amount of care, and to avoid providing too much or too little service.

Managed care companies build networks of providers, who discount the cost of their services to individuals insured under the managed care plan. They also agree to work within certain parameters. For example:

• Providers refer patients to hospitals within the same network.

• Providers generally prescribe medications that are covered by the plan. If a medication is not normally covered, providers must justify its use to the managed care company.

• Providers order tests on a judicious, case-by-case basis, rather than order the same group of tests for every patient.

Managed care companies review the work of their providers on a regular basis to ensure that these goals are met.

Managed care is nothing new—it has been around for almost a century. But it wasn't until the 1970s, when the federal government passed legislation in support of Health Maintenance Organizations (HMOs), that enrollment in managed care plans exploded. Today, three out of four Americans are covered by some type of managed care insurance.

The most common managed care plans are Health Maintenance Organizations (HMOs), Independent Practice Associations (IPAs), Preferred Provider Organizations (PPOs), and Point of Service Plans (POSs). As the consumer, you will need to understand the basic differences between the plans. How a plan is structured will make a difference in how and where you can obtain health care.

Health Maintenance Organizations

HMOs are pre-paid plans, which means that every month, the employer pays the managed care company a certain dollar amount for every employee. The managed care company uses this money to contract with groups of primary care physicians (PCPs). When the plan contracts with only one group, and directs all of its business to that group, it is called a "staff model" HMO. When the plan contracts with more than one group, the plan is called an Independent Practice Association (IPA) or Preferred Provider Organization (PPO).

Primary care physicians are paid a fixed monthly fee to deliver health care services to insured members. They also serve as "gatekeepers" to specialty services, which means that when you need to see a specialist (including a mental health professional), you must first ask the gatekeeper for a referral.

Critics of managed care systems view gatekeepers as obstacles to health care. They claim that PCPs are just another hoop to jump through, and some patients won't take the leap. This systematic thwarting of care, they charge, is what keeps health care costs down.

The gatekeeper's actual role is to keep costs down *while working in the best interests of the patient.* Gatekeepers do this in two ways. First, a gatekeeper assesses a patient's need to see a specialist. Many patients have become accustomed to automatically seeing a specialist for problems that could be handled just as effectively by a PCP. When specialists provide routine care, the overall cost of health care increases. Gatekeepers help control this by referring patients to a specialist only when necessary.

Second, when gatekeepers refer patients to a specialist, the specialist is typically a participating provider. Participating providers are clinicians who contract with HMOs. They agree to accept HMO fees and to practice health care in a manner that reflects managed care's clinical and financial goals.

It can be daunting to have to explain your mental health concerns to a gatekeeper physician, who is probably not going to treat the problem anyway. In response to these concerns, some states have passed legislation ordering health plans to allow direct access to the most frequently used specialists (like obstetricians, pediatricians, and gastrointestinal physicians).[2] Some HMOs are voluntarily dropping their gatekeeper requirement altogether, still others are streamlining the process to make it more efficient. Many HMOs now allow patients to obtain referrals over the phone.

Whether gatekeepers are successful—or even necessary—in keeping costs down remains a question. The Minnesota-based United Health Care Corporation, one of the largest managed care companies in the country, currently insures nearly two million people in eighteen states. It provides low-cost health care without the use of gatekeepers, and it plans to expand to several other states in 1997 and 1998.

In 1996, national enrollment in HMOs hovered around 27 percent—in other words, more than one in four insured individuals participated in an HMO. The average cost that year for an HMO-insured employee was $3,185. This was significantly lower than the cost to insure an employee under an indemnity plan, which averaged $3,739.[3]

Independent Practice Associations and Preferred Provider Organizations

IPAs and PPOs are groups of providers who contract with a managed care company to deliver services to enrollees at a discounted rate. Providers are only paid for the patients they see. This differs from HMOs, where providers are paid a monthly fee for each member.

An IPA or PPO is more flexible than a standard HMO, because consumers can usually see a participating provider without a referral from a gatekeeper physician.

At $3,293 per year, the 1996 average cost for a member enrolled in an IPA or PPO plan was higher than the cost of an HMO, but lower than the cost of a Point of Service Plan.[4]

Point of Service Plans

A Point of Service Plan (POS) is a combination of an indemnity plan and an HMO. In a POS, you—the consumer—decide whether or not to see someone within the network. If you choose someone within the plan's network, insurance will pay a higher percentage of your costs. If you choose someone outside of the network, insurance will pay a smaller percentage. The different rates of coverage are listed in your benefits handbook.

At $3,494 per year, the average cost to enroll an employee in a POS plan in 1996 was higher than an HMO, IPA, or PPO. Nevertheless, POS plans seem to be gaining popularity. In 1996, two-thirds of the individuals enrolled in managed care plans were enrolled in IPAs, PPOs, or POSs.[5] This suggests that employers prefer plans that offer more flexibility than standard HMOs. It will be interesting to see how the trend to relax gatekeeper requirements in HMOs will affect enrollment in POS plans over the next few years.

WHY IS MANAGED CARE CONTROVERSIAL?

Almost without exception, the introduction of managed care into new markets is like trial by fire—a painful process that most providers would prefer to avoid.

Why?

First, managed care challenges basic assumptions long held by traditional health care systems. Second, it emphasizes cost containment in an industry that, for decades, has avoided having to do so.

While concerns about managed care cut across the entire health care industry, the remainder of this chapter will focus on managed care as it relates to mental health services.

The Assumptions

Traditional reimbursement for mental health care was based on the following assumptions:

- Whatever the doctor says, goes.
- If some treatment is good, more is better.
- Everyone is entitled to the maximum amount of treatment available, regardless of its effectiveness.
- Cost is irrelevant, as long as the patient gets better.

The growth of managed care has systematically challenged these assumptions. When it comes to the type and amount of treatment, payers are unwilling to simply accept the opinion of providers. Instead, mental health clinicians must justify the choices they make.

For example, some clinicians think it is necessary to see patients twice a week or more, while others are comfortable seeing patients no more than once a week. What accounts for the difference? Is more treatment always better? What are the incentives for providers to see patients more frequently? Less frequently?

Another concern focuses on the level of care and the environment in which treatment takes place. Is hospitalization better than outpatient treatment? Is it even necessary? For whom? Why? Does more costly treatment produce better results? What is better? How do clinicians measure effectiveness?

These questions have had a tremendous effect on the mental health care industry, resulting in a shift in the balance of power. Mental health providers no longer make decisions about treatment alone; managed care firms have hired their own experts, whose opinions are sometimes at odds with traditional industry standards.

The concept of financial and clinical accountability is relatively new to some clinicians, and unwelcome. Many see it as an attempt by insurance companies to take control of patient care. Others view it is a threat to lucrative practices and comfortable lifestyles.

Not everybody is up in arms, however. Health care providers who understand the need for cost containment recognize two fundamental principles. First, some of the treatment for mental health problems is unnecessary or excessive. Second, if something isn't done to bring costs under control, patients and clinicians will eventually go broke. In terms of cost efficiency, the industry did little to regulate itself—even as it watched costs skyrocket out of control. It might as well have issued an invitation for a takeover. Now, the schism between those who accept the need for accountability and those who do not has created tension between managed care companies and clinicians, and among clinicians themselves.

The introduction of managed care into new geographic areas continues to be a difficult process. Therapists who are accustomed to running their own practices, setting their own prices, and choosing treatments do not relish working with managed care companies (or anybody else who asks too many questions about how, why, and what treatments are administered).

Standards of Care and Preferred Practices

If you break an arm, you go to a doctor to have it set. The doctor follows certain procedures to fix the arm. Chances are, a doctor in California will follow the same procedures as a doctor in Florida or New York. This is called a standard of care.

Standards of care are everywhere in medicine. They guide physicians in providing the most appropriate treatment for illnesses.

Standards of care do not exist like this in the mental health industry. If you decide to see a mental health professional for depression, your treatment will depend on the type of therapist you choose. For instance, a Marriage and Family therapist may view depression differently than a psychiatrist, who may treat the problem in a different way than a psychologist or social worker. In fact, five different professionals may treat the condition in five different ways.

Managed care and its supporters, however, have been advocating for the development and implementation of guidelines for clinical practice. Guidelines, they reason, would help clinicians know which treatments have been the most successful and cost effective. And while guidelines in mental health might not ever be as precise as they are for setting a broken bone, at least they would provide direction.

The movement toward preferred practices, or practice guidelines, is not without controversy. This is due, in part, to the many different types of therapists. A physician is a physician is a physician. But a therapist could be a psychologist, social worker, family therapist, psychiatrist, or nurse. The differences in training make it difficult to establish universal treatment guidelines. The establishment of guidelines is further hindered by therapists who view them as an effort by insurance companies to control mental health treatment.

How Does Managed Care "Manage" Behavioral Health Services?

First of all, it is important to recognize that not all managed care plans are created equal. Just as there are good and bad therapists, there are also good and bad managed care companies. Bad managed care companies provide poorly qualified reviewers (employees who keep track of the amount and quality of service for members), refuse to invest in their employees and networks, and do not take the time to understand the therapeutic communities into which they have moved. Good managed care companies provide leadership in the industry and place a balanced emphasis on quality of care and cost.

Quality

Product quality is as important in managed care as it is in any other industry. High-quality products drive satisfaction, and satisfaction drives customer base. Without a customer base, there is no business. A good managed care company pays attention to the product and the people who deliver it. It's the only way to stay in business. Quality, coupled with competitive pricing strategies, has resulted in the capture of nearly three-quarters of the health care market today.

The tools used to implement and monitor mental health care are credentialing, documentation, training, access to care, and case management.

Credentialing

Therapists who belong to a managed care network go through a credentialing process to ensure that they meet the standards of the health care plan. Each plan has its own credentialing process, so in areas where managed care is predominant, a therapist may be credentialed by a number of different plans.

In order to be credentialed, providers must be licensed by the state in which they are practicing and remain in good standing with the licensing board. Many plans will only work with providers who have practiced for five years or more, thus establishing a solid therapeutic base for members. Some companies work primarily with clinicians who have had formal training in brief therapies (see chapter 3).

Documentation

Managed care companies expect therapists to keep a record of pertinent information about each patient. A written record clearly explains a diagnosis and cites sufficient evidence to support it. It outlines the treatment plan and goals, and keeps track of the patient's progress. It also documents any correspondence the therapist has had with anyone else regarding the patient's care.

This formal record is a legal document as well as a method of communication. If a therapist were to get hit by a truck tomorrow, another therapist should be able to use the documentation to continue the patient's therapy.

Training

Ongoing training in the field of mental health is essential, regardless of the type of provider or the number of years in practice. As in other service industries, trends in mental health care are continuously changing. New techniques for improved care are being tested and developed, especially in managed care markets.

Many managed care firms sponsor ongoing training for network providers. They also encourage their participation in assessing which factors contribute to the success or failure of treatment.

Access to Care

Access to care is one of the most important issues in health care today. This is especially true in mental health services, where the need to see someone often involves a crisis situation.

Managed care companies expect their providers to be accessible to insured members. Providers often guarantee that new patients will be offered an appointment within seven days of their initial contact with the clinic. Some companies allow fourteen days, but anything beyond that is considered a substandard response. Fourteen days may seem like a long time, but there are a number of providers who cannot schedule a regular intake appointment for six to eight weeks.

If you are in crisis and need to talk to someone immediately, you should be able to do so. If you are in crisis during non-business hours, call your therapist—there should be a message machine or an answering service letting you know who you can call for help. Crisis numbers are also listed in your provider handbook.

Case Management

There are times when you may receive more than one type of service for your mental health concern. For instance, your therapist might ask you to see your regular physician to rule out any medical condition that could be causing your symptoms. He or she may also refer you to a psychiatrist to determine if there's a need for medication. The psychiatrist might refer you to a neurologist, who might ask you to schedule some tests with a neuropsychologist.

Case management refers to the monitoring and coordination of health care services. The goal of case management is to ensure that you are getting an adequate amount of treatment for your problems.

Therapists usually act as case managers, although some large clinics hire other professionals to coordinate health care services.

Many individuals have a medical condition as well as a behavioral condition—heart trouble and depression, for example. Again, when an individual sees several health care providers at once, it is important for a case manager to oversee and coordinate all aspects of care.

A medical condition can have a powerful influence on a mental health condition, and vice versa. Patients with cancer or other serious illnesses are often clinically anxious, for example, and anxiety can interfere with concentration, decision making, and general daily living. If you are dealing with a serious medical issue, discuss it with your therapist.

It is equally important to tell your physician if you are seeing a therapist, since medical problems often stem from psychiatric conditions. For example, symptoms such as numbness and tingling in the arms, sharp chest pains, shallow breathing, increased pulse, and rising blood pressure could indicate the presence of a panic disorder as well as a heart attack.

Symptoms common to both medical and psychiatric disorders include headaches, dizziness, lethargy, suppressed appetite, weight loss, weight gain, and vomiting. In order to treat the symptoms *and* the cause of your condition, both your therapist and physician need to know about your overall health. A case manager can help you receive the appropriate treatment from all of your health care providers.

Cost

Managed care companies use four strategies to control the costs of health care services: pre-certification, utilization review, fee negotiation, and the least restrictive environment.

Pre-certification

With most managed care plans, it is necessary to get approval before receiving clinical services. This is called pre-certification. It ensures that the treatment you are about to receive is necessary and falls within the guidelines of the plan.

For example, if you request outpatient therapy, your provider (or support staff at the provider's office) must call the managed care plan to verify your coverage and get permission to conduct an assessment.

If you request inpatient treatment, your therapist must call the managed care plan's hospital to explain why you should be admitted. If you do not have a therapist or a primary care physician, someone in the hospital's admission department or emergency room will determine if admission is necessary. They will then call the managed care plan, explain the situation, and request authorization for admission.

In a crisis situation, it is not always possible to contact your insurance company prior to admission. In this case, most companies expect to be contacted within twenty-four hours to certify inpatient treatment. Most hospitals will do this for you, but it's a good idea to ask. If no one calls your insurance company, payment might be delayed—or it might not be made at all.

Utilization Review

Managed care companies use a process called the utilization review (UR) to ensure that the mental health services you receive are necessary. Typically, a reviewer is a fully qualified Registered Nurse or a mental health clinician trained at the master's level.

Let's say you are seeing an outpatient therapist. The two of you feel you need more sessions than your insurance company had originally authorized. The therapist contacts the utilization reviewer assigned to your case. The reviewer looks at the treatment plan, treatment goals, progress to date, and other circumstances to determine if more sessions are necessary. Although UR is usually your therapist's responsibility, it is important that you know how many additional sessions have been approved. If you exceed the number of authorized visits, you may have to pay for them.

If you are receiving inpatient treatment, the reviewer will speak with your psychiatrist or the hospital's UR person every three to five days to ensure that they are following an authorized plan.

If you and your provider feel that you need more treatment, but the managed care company disagrees, you have the option of filing an appeal. Use it. An appeal reviewer may disagree with the first reviewer and grant your request.

Fees Negotiation

Managed care companies negotiate fees with their providers. Negotiated fees are sometimes lower than what providers normally charge, but providers generate more business by participating in a managed care network. This is an advantage in highly competitive health care markets.

Least Restrictive Environment

Behavioral health care is provided in four different settings, each one more restrictive (and expensive) than the next: outpatient, intensive outpatient, partial hospital (or day treatment), and inpatient. Managed care works to ensure that treatment is delivered in the least restrictive environment possible, which helps eliminate unnecessary costs.

Outpatient treatment takes place in the clinician's office, typically no more than once a week, depending on the type of care and the needs of the patient. For example, if you are taking medication, you might see the psychiatrist once every month or two to make sure that the medicine is working and to monitor side effects.

Outpatient visits occurring more than once a week qualify as Intensive Outpatient Treatment (IOP). This schedule is most commonly used in outpatient chemical dependence treatment programs, where sessions are held three or four times a week, usually in the evenings, for two to four hours per session.

Partial hospital programs, or day treatment programs, usually take place at a hospital. They typically require daily attendance. These programs are used to prevent patients from having to go into an inpatient setting. They can also ease the transition from an inpatient stay to an outpatient course of treatment.

Inpatient treatment is conducted on a psychiatric unit in a hospital. It provides twenty-four-hour supervision, daily visits from the psychiatrist, and various forms of group and individual therapy. Use of inpatient treatment has declined over the years, driven primarily by the growth of managed care. Problems that once required a hospital stay of thirty days or more can now be effectively treated in a less restrictive environment. Today, fewer patients are going into the hospital, and they are staying for shorter periods of time.

Inpatient treatment is reserved for the most severe problems—when it becomes apparent that a patient is incapable of caring for him- or herself. A hospital stay is meant to stabilize a crisis situation and ensure the patient's personal safety.

Although the information can be confusing at times, it's a good idea to learn what you can about your managed care plan. Familiarize yourself with your benefits—which services are covered, how they are delivered, and what they cost. The more knowledgeable you become about the resources available to you, the better informed you will be as a consumer.

NOTES

1. "Foster Higgens National Survey of Employer-Sponsored Health Plans 1996," (New York: A. Foster Higgens Company, 1997).

2. "Many HMOs Ease Rules Governing Visits to Specialists," *St. Paul Pioneer Press,* 2 February 1997.

3. "Foster Higgens National Survey of Employer-Sponsored Health Plans 1996."

4. Ibid.

5. Ibid.

CHAPTER FIVE

THE ASSESSMENT

You've picked your therapist and you're ready to take the plunge. Now what?

The first step in the therapeutic process is the assessment— the therapist's assessment of you, and more importantly, your assessment of the therapist.

Your assessment of a mental health clinician should be based on your gut reaction—the feeling you get from what is said, tone of voice, eye contact, level of empathy, keenness of interest, and the therapist's overall ability to connect with you.

If the therapeutic relationship is going to work, you should get the sense that the therapist understands what you are saying. He or she should help you feel comfortable enough to talk about uncomfortable issues, even secrets. To trust your therapist, you must believe that he or she is competent. Competence does not mean having the answers to all your problems. It means having the ability to help you discover your own solutions.

Finally, it is important that you feel your therapist respects you, and that you respect your therapist. You do not have to like your therapist. Remember, this is a paid relationship—you are not looking for friendship here. Your decision to work with a particular therapist will depend largely on whether you think the two of you can work together as a team.

While you are assessing your therapist, the therapist will be assessing you in order to make a diagnosis.

Apart from establishing a workable relationship, the therapist must complete five tasks during an assessment:

- Identify the "presenting problem"
- Gather family history and other relevant information
- Identify current symptoms
- Estimate the effect of symptoms on your ability to carry on with a daily routine
- Make a diagnosis

This is a lot to do in a short period of time. It requires organization on the clinician's part, and a willingness to be forthcoming on yours.

Presenting Problem

The presenting problem is the main reason you decided to seek help. Presenting problems fall into one of three categories: acute, chronic, or a combination of the two.

Acute

Generally, acute problems are problems that occur suddenly, out of the blue. They are so distressing that they interrupt the flow of daily activity. An acute problem looks and feels like a crisis. It catches you off guard. This leads to feelings of confusion, loss of control, hopelessness, helplessness. It is the sense of "not knowing what to do" that often prompts the first call to a mental health professional.

For example, if Lisa from chapter 1 were to seek professional help, her presenting problem would be the sudden death of a very good friend—a totally unpredictable event with far-reaching implications. Lisa was faced with a devastating loss. As time went on, she also faced the disappointment of not getting the much-needed support from her family, who wanted her to get over Tracy's death.

The loss of a loved one, be it through death or divorce, is one of the most common events to prompt an individual to seek professional help. Other acute problems include:

- Partner having an affair
- Child failing in school
- Major argument with a family member or good friend
- Diagnosis of a serious illness
- Job loss
- Arrest for drunk driving
- Sudden, major legal problems
- Assault or rape

Chronic

Problems of a long-standing nature are said to be chronic. They may have been around for months, even years. Some problems are so entrenched you can barely remember life without them.

Individuals who seek help for chronic problems are driven by frustration (that feeling of wanting to tear your hair out) or fatigue (the sense that you can't go on).

Don't be discouraged. Change doesn't happen unless you hurt enough, and when you hurt enough, you become frustrated, fatigued, or both. From a clinical perspective, this is good news for both you and your therapist, because it signals a readiness for change.

Frustration is an energy-producing emotion. Its by-products include anger, aggravation, and outrage—all of which can motivate you to get the help you need.

Fatigue, on the other hand, is an overarching sense of being "too tired" to face the problem alone anymore. It drains your energy, resulting in lethargy, apathy, and inertia. Sometimes you want to give up altogether. Like getting a leg cramp in the deep end of the pool, fatigue is a sign that it's time to come out of the water.

Sometimes, frustration and fatigue lead to a gradual wearing away of energy and spirit. Julie, the sales manager from chapter 1, is a good example. Her frustration with her boss left her too tired to do the things she used to enjoy. Frustration and fatigue wore her down until she had no other choice but to change her situation.

Some of the more common chronic problems include:
- Inability to develop healthy friendships
- Poor choice of romantic partners
- Nervousness and anxiety
- Repetitive, compulsive behaviors
- Recurring thoughts that are difficult to push away
- Feelings of jealousy, rage, anger
- Lack of self-confidence; poor self-esteem

Acute Combined with Chronic

An acute problem piled on top of a chronic one is a double-whammy—it can result in a partial or total shutdown.

David, the computer-business owner from chapter 1, shows how an acute situation underscores the effects of long-standing difficulties. Karen's abrupt departure brought certain chronic emotions to the surface for David—jealousy, insecurity, a need for control. If Karen hadn't left him, he would not have sought help. Her action forced him to look at his long-standing behaviors.

The following examples show how acute problems can intersect chronic ones:

• Constant feelings of jealousy ignite upon learning that a partner is having an affair

• Poor self-esteem deepens after an assault

• Chronic obsession about money and financial security becomes paralyzing when threatened with job loss

• Difficulty forming new relationships is underscored when a close friend dies

• A child's failure in school heightens chronic feelings of low self-esteem

In some cases, the presenting problem is the reason a patient seeks help. In others, it's just the tip of the iceberg. Either way, the presenting problem is an important part of the therapist's assessment, and a very good place to start.

GATHERING INFORMATION

After you describe your presenting problem, your therapist will ask a series of questions about your life, your symptoms, and your ability to carry on with everyday activities. The exact nature of these questions will depend on your presenting problem and the type of therapist.

For instance, if the presenting problem is a crisis, most of the session will focus on assessing your level of personal safety, and helping you find ways to manage the crisis situation. Your therapist will help you determine what support you might need outside of therapy, and how you might obtain it. He or she will also discuss plans to ensure your physical safety. When necessary, the therapist will direct you to other services (such as a hospital or shelter).

In noncrisis situations, questions are more apt to reflect the clinician's training. For example, a psychiatrist will ask questions related to your physical health and abilities, your past and current medical problems, and your experience with medications. A family therapist is more likely to inquire about communication patterns and relationships in your family. He or she will also ask if any significant events or disturbances occurred while you were growing up, such as the death of a parent, removal from your home, or unconventional living arrangements, like foster care or an orphanage.

Family History

Your therapist will ask you questions about your family history in order to put your problems into context. This will help the therapist understand your family's patterns—how members communicated, dealt with conflict, solved problems, and supported each other. You will probably be invited to talk about the following:

- Your relationship with your parents
- Methods of discipline used (specifically, the use of force)
- Alcohol or other drug use by family members, including parents
- Financial problems
- Serious illness among family members, including hospitalizations for psychiatric problems and time spent in state hospitals
- History of sexual abuse by family or non-family member
- History of rape or other forms of assault
- Performance in school
- Relationships with friends
- Any counseling sought and why

CURRENT SYMPTOMS

Symptoms tell us when something is wrong. They can be physical, emotional, or psychological, and they are measured by their frequency, intensity, and duration.

Symptoms may involve the sudden appearance of thoughts, feelings, and behaviors that don't normally occur, or the disappearance of thoughts, feelings, and behaviors that normally do.

Let's say your partner has just admitted to having an affair. You feel like you've been hit by a train. You cry all the time, want to throw up at the sight of food, have a hard time getting out of bed in the morning, and couldn't read a magazine cover to cover if your life depended on it. Your normal ability to concentrate has vanished. The crying, nausea, and trouble getting up in the morning are new behaviors.

Any sudden, radical change is a symptom worth mentioning to your therapist, even if it does not appear to be related to your presenting problem.

Your therapist will ask if you are having any physical symptoms. Patients experiencing significant physical symptoms will probably be asked to see a family doctor to rule out the possibility of a medical problem as the source of discomfort.

If you have already been diagnosed with a medical problem, make sure you let the therapist know. Sometimes the symptoms of medical problems mimic those of psychological problems, and vice versa (see page 91). The more information you give your therapist, the more accurate his or her diagnosis will be.

EFFECTS OF SYMPTOMS

Your therapist will attempt to determine the severity of your symptoms based on how they affect your daily routine. Some symptoms can significantly impair your ability to function. If your partner is having an affair, the symptoms might be incapacitating. But not everyone responds to events in the same manner, and not all symptoms are quite so dramatic. The effects vary from person to person.

Your therapist will ask questions about your life prior to the onset of the current problem. This will help the therapist determine how much of your change in thinking, feeling, and behavior can be attributed to your current situation, and how much was already there before. This information will aid the therapist in his or her diagnosis.

Other Assessment Tools

In some cases, the therapist may ask you to see a psychiatrist or a psychologist before making a diagnosis.

Referral to a Psychiatrist

A therapist may refer you to a psychiatrist to obtain a second opinion about a diagnosis, and to determine whether medication would be helpful. If you are referred to a psychiatrist, find out why. Your therapist should give you an explanation.

Your therapist will also ask how you feel about taking medication. Be honest about this. There is a 50-50 chance that the psychiatrist will recommend medicine. If you are at all willing to consider the possibility of taking medication, then by all means, follow through with the referral.

By agreeing to see a psychiatrist, you simply agree to discuss your problems with a specially trained medical doctor, get feedback on your condition, and listen to the recommendation. You are not required to follow the recommendation.

If You Are Willing to Consider Medication

Before you visit the psychiatrist, write down the names of any medications you are currently taking and what they are for. Give this list to the psychiatrist. If you have ever been prescribed medicine to help with mood or thinking, say so. Be sure to mention the name of the medicine.

If the psychiatrist prescribes medication, he or she should explain why, what it does, what the side effects are, and whether there are special instructions to follow. Ask questions—how it works, how long you will need to take it, whether there are any dietary restrictions—and make sure you understand the answers.

As a general rule, you should not use alcohol or other drugs while taking medication. If you drink or use drugs, let the psychiatrist know. It may make a difference in the type and dosage of medication, and whether or not it is even prescribed.

After you have been taking the medicine for a short period of time, you will be asked to return to the psychiatrist for follow-up visits. The interval between visits will depend on the type of medication and the psychiatrist's preference. You may be asked to come in frequently (weekly or every other week) until the psychiatrist is confidant about the medication's effect. Once you are stable—that is, once the medication is doing what it's supposed to do—you will probably only need to come in every two or three months.

If You Are Unwilling to Consider Medication

If you are opposed to taking medication, tell your therapist. The therapist will probably want to explore your objections, answer your questions, and dispel any myths you may have so you better understand why and how medication may be helpful.

One of the most common concerns among individuals who refuse psychotropic medication (drugs that target thoughts, feelings, and behaviors) is fear of addiction. One of the reasons behind this fear is the effect of public information campaigns urging people to live a "drug-free" lifestyle. Many individuals interpret "drug free" to mean "medication free" as well.

Some people feel that taking medication to improve their mood is tantamount to cheating. Others fear that if the medicine really does help, they may not want to stop taking it. While self-sufficiency is admirable in many circumstances, it is not in the case of psychotropic medication. Emotional problems frequently stem from a biological base, such as a chemical imbalance in the brain. Just as insulin corrects a malfunctioning pancreas, psychotropic medicine will often correct emotion and mood malfunctions.

Of course, there are those who believe that a drug is a drug is a drug, and all drugs are potentially addicting. This is simply not true. In fact, none of the medications commonly used to treat depression or thought disorders (such as psychosis or schizophrenia) are addicting. There are some medicines used to treat anxiety that can be addictive when used excessively or for extended periods of time, but in those and all other cases, the psychiatrist will review all possible side effects with the patient beforehand, including potential for addiction.

The propensity for addiction varies from patient to patient. Some people are predisposed to addiction. For example, if one of your parents was an alcoholic, you have a greater chance of becoming an alcoholic yourself. Depending on the biological makeup of each individual, one drug given to two different people may have two very different effects.

People who have a history of drug abuse are often more wary of psychotropic medication than those who do not. Individuals being treated for chemical dependency, for example, frequently refuse to consider prescribed medications. This can cause problems later on, mainly because many of these people have histories of depression and anxiety. When depression and anxiety go untreated, there is a greater chance that a chemically dependent person will return to drug use. With proper use of psychotropic medication, however, this risk can be reduced.

If, after careful consideration, you are still not interested in trying medication, decline your therapist's referral to a psychiatrist. There is no sense in putting yourself in a situation where you might feel coerced into doing something you don't want to do. Your time and energy are valuable, as are the psychiatrist's.

Generally, the most effective treatments are the ones you agree to.

Referral to a Psychologist

There are literally hundreds of tests designed to determine a wide range of psychological characteristics. It is not uncommon for a therapist to refer patients to a psychologist for testing, but the tests should relate to a question about a patient's ability to carry on with his or her daily activities. Therapists order these tests when they have specific diagnostic questions in mind. The most common questions relate to:

- Personality or quality of thinking
- Type and quality of mood
- Cognitive ability

If you do not understand why your therapist has requested psychological testing, ask. He or she should explain how the results will be used to make a diagnosis.

Tests in a mental health setting may be self-administered or administered by a psychologist. Self-administered tests are written tests that come in a variety of formats. Some are fill-in-the-blanks, others are rating scales. Still others are multiple choice and come with computer score sheets. Certain tests can be taken on a computer at the clinic, with the psychologist's permission. Nearly all tests need to be taken in the therapist's office. You cannot bring a test home. Taking a test at home may render it invalid.

I learned this the hard way many years ago when I first began my clinical work. I had asked an adolescent client of mine to take an MMPI (Minnesota Multiphasic Personality Inventory), a common, but rather lengthy, personality test. She lived quite a distance from the clinic, and her mother was disgruntled about having to drive her back "just to take a test." I was young, unsure of myself, and eager to make my clients' lives as simple as possible, so I relented.

When my client returned the next week, I asked her how the test went. She said fine. Her mother, however, rolled her eyes and said her daughter had just finished the test on the way over, and had asked several times about how to answer the questions. She also explained that her daughter had called a number of friends to help her take the test.

Besides the propensity to ask for help, there are other distractions at home: the telephone, friends, kids, homework, laundry, dinner, dishes, and even cleaning the bathroom, if you're really desperate for a diversion.

Most tests must be completed in one sitting, which is another reason for taking tests at a clinic. Because psychological tests are a measure of functioning at a particular point in time, tests taken over extended periods of time may produce questionable results.

A third problem with take-home tests involves a possible breach of security. Test creators spend months and years making sure a test measures what it's supposed to measure. If the contents of the test are made public, future test results would be considered contaminated and potentially worthless, rendering the entire test of dubious value.

The following is a list of the most common psychological tests. If your therapist asks you to take any of these tests, he or she should explain what the test will reveal, and how that information will be used in your treatment.

Personality / Quality of Thinking	
Rorschach	"Inkblot test"
Thematic Apperception Test (TAT)	Picture-telling test
Minnesota Multiphasic Personality Inventory (MMPI 2)	True-false personality test
Minnesota Multiphasic Personality Inventory A (MMPI A)	True-false personality test for adolescents
Roberts Apperception Test	Picture-telling test
Myers-Briggs	Personality test
Millon Clinical Multiaxial Inventory III	Personality test
House-Tree-Person	Drawing test

Mood	
Beck Depression Inventory (BDI)	Rating scale
Beck Anxiety Scale (BAS)	Rating scale
Beck Hopelessness Scale (BHS)	True-false test
Revised Hamilton Rating Scale for Depression	Rating scale
Eating Disorders Inventory (EDI)	Symptom checklist
Minnesota Multiphasic Personality Inventory (MMPI 2)	True-false personality test

Cognitive Ability	
Wechsler Adult Intelligence Scale–Revised (WAIS–R)	Intelligence test
Wechsler Memory Scale– Revised (WMS–R)	Memory test
Bender Visual Motor Gestalt	Test of visual perception
Luria-Nebraska Neuropsychological Battery	Collection of tests for cognitive functioning

The Philosophy of Testing

In the old days (when money was no object), it was common for patients to take several hours' worth of tests even before their first appointment with a therapist. Mental health clinics routinely ordered a standard battery of tests on all patients, regardless of the presenting problem.

There were several difficulties with this approach. First, it took a great deal of time to administer and complete the tests. Second, there was no attempt to focus on a specific problem. Ordering a standard battery was akin to having a medical doctor x-ray every part of the body, rather than just the one part that hurt. Third, it was expensive to administer, score, interpret, and report on these tests. Without a solid diagnostic question in mind, this "shot gun" approach to assessment might have been interesting, but not very effective.

Today, most insurance companies will only pay for tests that are necessary to diagnose or treat a patient. Therefore, the question the tests are supposed to address must be clearly formulated before costs will be reimbursed.

Testing and Insurance

Before you agree to see a psychiatrist or psychologist, ask your therapist if insurance will cover it. Also, keep in mind that visits to these specialists may require pre-certification before insurance will pay the costs. Protect yourself—when you make the appointment to see a psychiatrist or psychologist, ask about pre-certification requirements at the same time. If you do not receive pre-certification, insurance will probably not reimburse the cost.

THE DIAGNOSIS

The assessment phase ends once the therapist has established a working diagnosis—usually somewhere between the first and fourth visit. The diagnosis serves as the foundation for a treatment plan and goals.

Your therapist will make a diagnosis using one of two diagnostic systems: *International Classification of Diseases, Ninth Edition (ICD-9)*, or the *Diagnostic and Statistical Manual of Mental Disorders, Fourth Edition (DSM-IV)*. The remainder of this discussion will focus on the *DSM-IV*, since it is the more popular of the two, especially with managed care reviewers.

There are five parts to a diagnosis. Each part, or axis, communicates a wealth of information about the patient. This system was designed to help clinicians view patients in a more holistic manner. It is nothing more than a way to organize information obtained during the assessment.

Axis One: Clinical Conditions

A clinical disorder is usually the principal reason for your visit to the therapist. For example, if you are having problems with mood, anxiety, drugs, an eating disorder, sexual difficulties, or a relationship issue, this information will be recorded on the first axis. Other problems noted here might include sleep disorders, phobias, pathological gambling, post-traumatic stress disorder, thought problems (including dementia, delirium, and psychosis), and problems first identified in childhood (such as attention deficit disorder and conduct disorder).

Axis Two: Personality Disorders

A personality disorder is an inflexible, ongoing pattern of perception or behavior that causes distress or impairment. These perceptions and behaviors fall outside of cultural expectations. They first become evident in adolescence or early adulthood. Some of the more common personality disorders include the following:

Disorder	Behavioral Characteristic
Dependent	Clingy, submissive; excessive need to be taken care of
Antisocial	Disregards and violates the rights of others; sometimes violent
Borderline	Impulsive; highly unstable interpersonal relationships and self-image
Avoidant	Socially inhibited; hypersensitive to negative comments; feels inadequate
Histrionic	Excessively emotional and attention seeking
Paranoid	Suspicious; thinks others are out to cause him or her harm

Axis Three: Medical Conditions

Any significant medical problems, past or current, are recorded on this axis. Because medical conditions can have a profound effect on mood, thought, and behavior, their notation is especially important for setting goals and planning treatment. Commonly noted medical conditions include cancer, lupus, multiple sclerosis, cardiac disease, chronic pain, diabetes, HIV, AIDS, thyroid disease, respiratory problems, and chronic obstructive pulmonary disease (COPD). Medical problems that cause any degree of impairment (or potential impairment) will be noted on axis three.

Axis Four: Stressors

In this section, the therapist records ongoing stressors that might effect a patient's daily routine. Stressors include legal problems, serving as the primary caregiver for an aging parent, the death of a family member or close friend, or extreme difficulties with finances, education, or housing.

Noting environmental problems helps place the patient's current difficulties in a context. For example, if a patient is suffering from anxiety, it would help the therapist to know that he is the sole caregiver for his dying mother, and is struggling to make ends meet financially while trying to encourage a highly anxious child to attend school every day. In this case, his environmental stressors may very well be the origins of the patient's anxiety. By placing problems in context, therapists can design a more efficient treatment plan.

Axis Five: Overall Functioning

The Global Assessment of Functioning (GAF) score is a rating on a scale from 1 to 100. The higher the number, the healthier the individual. For example, individuals who are unable to maintain basic personal hygiene, have attempted suicide with the clear intention of dying, or are in danger of harming themselves might receive a GAF score of 10. A GAF score of 50 indicates a person who might have notable obsessions or compulsions; serious thoughts of suicide; or an inability to function at home, school, or work.

A clinician will usually assign two GAF scores to a patient, such as 25/80. The first score indicates the patient's level of functioning at the time of the assessment. The second score shows the patient's highest level of functioning within the past year, which gives the clinician (and any reviewer) an idea of how well the patient was doing at his or her best. Progress can be measured at the end of treatment, or anytime throughout.

If you have questions about the diagnosis, be sure to ask. Part of being a good patient is a willingness to actively participate in your own treatment. This means asking questions about things you don't understand. You may not always get the answers you like—or like the answers you get—but your treatment will be far more successful and gratifying if you know the general results of your assessment and how those results be used.

CHAPTER SIX

TREATMENT PLANS
AND TREATMENT GOALS

*"If we don't know the direction
in which we are headed, we just might end up there."*
—Old Chinese proverb

In therapy, success depends on your expectations. Most clients expect to leave therapy feeling better than they did when they came in. Others seek explanations for confusing or troubling situations. Some want to make changes in their own behavior, still others hope to change the behavior of family members, friends, or partners.

Part of the therapist's job is to help identify and define a successful course of treatment for every client who crosses the therapeutic threshold. This means setting treatment goals and designing a treatment plan to achieve those goals.

As discussed in chapter 3, therapies can be divided according to anticipated length of treatment: long-term therapy and brief therapy. Therapists who have been trained in methods of long-term therapy have a vastly different set of assumptions from those trained in brief therapy.

For example, therapists who work on a long-term basis assume a successful course of treatment requires anywhere from several months to several years. Brief therapists believe that many goals can be accomplished in as little as a couple of months. The estimated length of treatment largely depends on how the therapist perceives the purpose and process of therapy.

Long-term therapists see therapy as a way to identify and correct fundamental errors that occurred during various phases of development. For example, clients who had neglectful or abusive parents may need to be reparented.

Brief therapists are more interested in the *effects* of certain life experiences. Unlike long-term therapy, which attempts to go back and redo basic errors, brief therapy helps clients handle the aftermath, teaching them healthier ways of compensating for what might have been lost or destroyed.

Brief therapists provide solution-focused treatment. Their emphasis is on finding a way to resolve or manage a specific problem. Most types of therapy can be modified to fit the brief therapy model, including psychodynamic therapy and family therapy.

There is no definitive evidence to suggest that more therapy is necessarily better. Furthermore, brief therapy is more cost efficient than long-term therapy. For these reasons, brief therapies have become the mainstay of managed care.

Therapists who practice brief therapy make several assumptions about their clients:[1]

Most people who seek help from mental health professionals are capable of solving or managing their problems.

A solution-focused therapist will help you identify your problem-solving skills. He or she will also teach you new skills, so you can practice them throughout the course of your treatment.

Long-term therapy is more deficit driven than brief therapy—it tends to focus almost solely on what is not working, rather than what is. When our skills and strategies are not enough to overcome challenges, these deficits cause pain and sometimes dysfunction. Predictably, our deficits become the focus of attention.

Solution-focused therapy is not just about deficits. It is also about strengths. A therapist's ability to perceive your strengths is critical to the success of your treatment.

Unfortunately, not all therapists are trained to look for strengths in their clients. Strengths are indicators of health and wellness; mental health clinicians study pathology and illness. While it is necessary that therapists understand psychological illness, it is equally important that they acknowledge the "health" part of "mental health." All too often, mental health is defined simply as the absence of anything seriously wrong.

Solution-focused therapists understand that strengths can often be used in the service of deficits. Clients themselves are a tremendous resource; they bring their own expertise into therapy. An intuitive therapist will know how to help clients use their own strengths to their advantage.

Clients want help with specific problems, not global ones.

Most patients find it difficult to articulate their problems at first. They begin with broad complaints like, "I'm not happy," "I'm depressed," or "My marriage is a mess." Solution-focused therapists believe that clients want help with more specific problems, so they ask questions to help clients define their problems more clearly.

Let's say you're feeling depressed and overwhelmed, but you're not sure why. Your therapist asks you to describe how it feels to be "depressed" and "overwhelmed," and when you first noticed these feelings. She then has you talk about your work, family relationships, outside activities, and significant changes in your life.

You start to realize that your depression began about three months after your mother moved into a condominium a mile away from you. Since then, she has been quite generous with advice on how to handle the children, finances, housework, your husband, and even your job. She calls daily to give her opinion on everything from the color of your son's hair to the length of your front lawn. The mere sound of her voice over the phone puts your stomach in knots. She *is* your mother, but that doesn't make you feel any better.

Feeling depressed and overwhelmed is a global problem. It seems much too big to handle. But with the help of your therapist, you are able to break it down into smaller, more manageable concerns. By the end of the assessment phase, you have identified the following specific problems, as well as corresponding treatment goals:

Problem: I get irritated with my mother's daily phone calls.
Treatment Goal: Design a way to handle the calls differently.

Problem: I let my mother "walk all over me."
Treatment Goal: Learn specific assertiveness strategies.

Problem: I can't eat, sleep, or concentrate, I cry frequently, and I've lost ten pounds in two months.
Treatment Goal: Obtain an evaluation for medication.

Clients want to improve as quickly as possible. They are more interested in living than in continuing therapy.

Chances are, you're wondering, "How long will I have to keep coming to therapy?" Solution-focused therapists believe that most clients are interested in dealing with their problems in a time-efficient manner so they can get on with life. This is why you are treated as an active participant in therapy, rather than a passive recipient.

Your therapist is likely to give you homework to do outside of your sessions. In fact, solution-focused therapists believe that the real work of therapy—observing yourself, experimenting with different decisions, trying new strategies, and testing the waters of change—occurs between sessions. Therapy sessions are simply the springboard for these changes.

The solution-focused therapist views therapy as a tool, not a way of life. When used correctly, therapy can help you shape choices and decisions that will gradually improve your quality of life.

Therapy is developmental.

Therapy is a developmental process, which means it is most helpful during periods of change. Change comes about in two ways—through naturally occurring transitions in the life cycle, or through sudden, unexpected events. Whether positive or negative, change creates a major disruption in our lives, resulting in a sense of being off balance.

Natural Transitions

For many people, any change is difficult. The transition from one phase of life to another can be bumpy, even when the transition was desired and planned.

For example, most adults see having a baby as a positive event. The anticipation and excitement are tremendous. But the expectations are unrealistic at times, and the transition from calm, joyful anticipation to a hectic, sleep-deprived reality can be strenuous. This stress often comes as a surprise.

Other natural transitions include:

• Marriage (or formalizing a relationship)
• Divorce (or breaking up)
• "Empty nest" (when children leave home and move into adulthood)
• Caring for an aging parent
• Death of a parent

Aside from the obvious changes they bring, these natural transitions in life create stress and vulnerability, which often prompt individuals to seek professional help.

Unexpected Events

Whether positive or negative, unexpected events can bring significant change. A positive life-altering event might be a promotion, job offer from another company, or financial windfall (from an inheritance or the lottery, for example). Negative life-altering events include serious accidents, the loss of a job or business, serious illness, or the loss of a loved one.

Transitions involving loss are especially difficult to manage. They challenge our perceptions, beliefs, values, and understanding. Such transitions demand that we find ways to accept our loss and somehow go on with life.

Many people seek therapy after they experience a loss. Dealing with loss can be overwhelming. It affects many people around the suffering individual, and it takes an unsuspecting toll on relationships, even healthy ones. When one or both partners experience a loss, their grief magnifies differences in coping styles as well as existing conflict within the relationship. This is why it is not uncommon to see a good marriage fall apart after the death of a child.

Treatment is intermittent.

Therapy generally occurs within the context of pain. Solution-focused therapists believe that when pain subsides or becomes more manageable, and when thoughts, feelings, and behaviors have changed for the better, treatment ends—at least for the time being.

Unlike long-term therapy, where patients are seen continuously whether or not there is an urgent need, solution-focused treatment views therapy as an episode of care. Each episode has a beginning, middle, and end, and occurs on an as-needed basis. Episodes of care empower clients to take what they learn and go forward, helping them build confidence and skills and encouraging them toward a life of independence.

Because solution-focused therapy is intermittent, clients often return for additional episodes of treatment. This is to be expected—solution-focused therapists assume clients may not resolve all their problems in a single episode of care.

For long-term therapists, treatment is more like a cake—either it is done, or it is not. If clients return for more therapy, the first course of treatment may be considered a failure. Long-term therapy is more likely to encourage overreliance on the therapist and the therapy process. This can be a problem for clients who gravitate toward dependent relationships.

Treatment is best delivered in the least restrictive setting possible.

The levels of care discussed in chapter 4—outpatient, intensive outpatient, partial hospital, and inpatient—run on a continuum from least restrictive to most restrictive.

Solution-focused therapists, as well as proponents of managed care, believe that therapeutic intervention should occur in the least restrictive environment possible. For example, if you can be treated in a partial hospital program instead of an inpatient unit, then partial hospital is the preferred level of treatment. If an out-patient setting would be as effective as a partial hospital program, then outpatient treatment is the preferred setting.

There are a number of reasons for this. First, the more restrictive the environment, the more removed you are from familiar sur-roundings—and the support those surroundings afford. If you can remain in your own environment, you are more likely to obtain help, guidance, and feedback from the people you know and trust.

Second, there is no clinical evidence to support the idea that restrictive levels of intervention are more effective than less-restrictive levels (except in the most severe cases).

Third, less-restrictive levels of care are more economical. Many policies have dollar or session limits on inpatient and outpatient care. Once these dollars or sessions are exhausted, options for treat-ment are limited to what you can pay for yourself.

Let's say that your symptoms are so severe that your therapist believes you need more intensive treatment than your current week-ly schedule. After a careful assessment, he or she determines that a partial hospital program or an inpatient stay would be more effective than outpatient care. Together you decide that the partial program is preferable. You attend the partial program all day, every day, but return home in the evenings. Your insurance policy covers 80 percent of the cost. You pay the other 20 percent.

The economics of the situation are important, especially if you have a 20 percent co-payment. If you had participated in the inpatient program, your bed would have cost $1,000 per day. Your portion would have been $200 per day. The average length of stay in an inpatient setting is about seven days, which would have cost $1,400 out of your own pocket.

The partial hospital program costs roughly one-third of the inpatient program, or about $350 per day. With your 20 percent co-payment, you would pay $70 per day, or $490 for the entire seven days. Still pricey, but it's more reasonable than inpatient treatment.

We live in a society where more is believed to be better. This is not necessarily the case in the mental health industry, where the goal of treatment is to increase your ability to carry on from day to day—and *decrease* your reliance on mental health services.

TREATMENT GOALS

A treatment goal is a destination, like an endpoint to a trip. It is the place you want to be when you have completed your course of therapy.

Establishing clear and specific treatment goals is something of an art—the usual tendency is to define goals too broadly. Although broad goals are a good place to start, they are not a good place to end. Goals need to be explicit if they are to be meaningful. Treatment that wanders too far afield can be frustrating and ineffective.

Identifying a broad treatment goal is like deciding to drive to Arizona. You have a general idea of which direction to go, but once you get to the border, you'll need to clarify your expectations. If you want to see the gorgeous red rock of Sedona but end up in a traffic jam in Phoenix instead, you're likely to be disappointed.

Explicit treatment goals do not have to be inflexible. Goals can and do change along the way. Let's say that on the way to Arizona, you decide that what you really want is to get a good look at the Mississippi River and shop at the Mall of America. You rechart your course, take a sharp turn, and head straight for Minneapolis.

When shifting your goals, be sure that both you and your therapist are aware of the shift and why it is taking place.

Defining Treatment Goals

During your first few sessions, you and the therapist will define your treatment goals. Your treatment goals will be directly related to the diagnosis. This is true in medical care as well. If you go to your family doctor with an upper respiratory infection, you would not expect to be treated for a sprained ankle.

The link between goals and diagnosis provides a context for treatment. This is essential from a financial perspective. When your insurance company decides whether to pay for your therapy, it checks to make sure that your goals are related to the diagnosis.

Keeping Goals Realistic

When they first enter therapy, many patients are focused on changing the people around them. This is unrealistic. The purpose of therapy is to focus on what you want to change about yourself. Your therapist will help you define precisely what it is about yourself you want to change, and together you can set realistic goals for treatment.

For example, David, the computer consultant from chapter 1, spent most of his first session complaining about his wife's behavior. The therapist worked to help David focus on himself instead. The following are excerpts from David's first session in therapy.

Therapist: So you're here today because of your wife's note saying she was leaving until you, or the two of you, got some help.

David: Yeah, but she knows that if she just wasn't so busy, everything would be okay, like it was before she started school.

Therapist: So the relationship was better before she decided to return to school?

David: Much better.

Therapist: All couples have their fights, no matter how good the marriage might be. What kind of things did the two of you argue about?

David: Just the little, usual stuff—you know, like whether to rent an apartment or buy a house, what part of town we should live in, furniture—you know, stuff like that.

Therapist: What would happen during your arguments?

David: Oh, not much. She would usually pick a fight because she didn't like the decisions I made. Like she really got ticked off when I bought that lot for us to build a house on—I thought it was perfect. But she started in on me about how unfair it was for me to buy something like that without her looking at it—almost like she thinks I need her approval! Well, I don't. So then I got mad.

Therapist: What do you usually do when you get mad?

David: Well, that's another thing that bothers her. She doesn't like it when I get mad.

Therapist: How would she know if you were mad? What sort of things do you normally do?

David: Oh, I lose my temper sometimes and yell at her. I suppose there's been a couple of times when I've called her a few names I shouldn't have, but I can't help it.

Therapist: What else do you do when you're mad?

David: Well, when I get really mad, I'll throw something.

Therapist: Throw something?

David: Yeah, like a dish or a lamp—but I usually don't hurt anyone, and I've never done it in front of her. Once I punched a hole in the wall. Another time I accidentally dented the fender of her car when I kicked it. I threw a chair just before I came here, and a couple of glasses that were sitting on the table broke—that's the first time I've ever really broken anything. I've never hit her though, and I know I never would. My dad used to slap my mom around, and I know I'd never do that.

Therapist: How do you know?

David: I just know. Anyway, I feel bad about all that stuff. I don't like it, but I can't help it.

Therapist: Ever think that would be something you might want to change? Figuring out a different way to deal with your anger?

David: Yeah, I guess I've thought about it, but I don't know how.

By the end of three sessions, David's therapist had diagnosed him as having partner-relationship problems, as well as an intermittent explosive disorder (the urge to act aggressively, which often leads to assault or destruction of property).

The therapist reviewed his findings with David, explaining the diagnosis and different treatment options. Then he asked David to make a list of goals for therapy.

When David returned for his next session, he brought the following list with him.

David's Goals for Therapy

- To get my wife back
- To have her not spend so much time with other men
- To control my temper
- To stop throwing stuff, punching walls, etc., when I'm mad

Two of the goals were directed at changing his wife's behavior, and two focused on changing his own. The therapist reminded David that it was more realistic to set treatment goals for himself than to set goals aimed at changing his wife.

David wasn't happy with this. "If you can't help me get her back, what am I doing here?" Little by little, however, the therapist helped David understand three things:

1. The only behavior he'd be able to control was his own.

2. Regardless of what happened between David and his wife, he needed to change the way he expressed his anger.

3. He could express his anger differently by finding healthier ways of communicating.

Once David understood that he was responsible for his own behavior and the way he expressed his feelings, he could set realistic treatment goals—goals that focused on changing *his* behavior. Then, he and his therapist could focus on how David could meet those treatment goals.

TREATMENT PLANS

If the treatment goal is the final destination, the treatment plan is the map that tells you how to get there. If you knew how to get there on your own, chances are you wouldn't be in therapy. But it's difficult to chart your course when you're in the middle of a storm. That's where the therapist comes in. Therapists design treatment plans to help clients meet their treatment goals.

Most people identify more than one treatment goal. When goals are so similar that they overlap, they can be grouped together and treated as one (for example, "to improve self-esteem" or "to be more confident"). Goals that are dissimilar need to be prioritized. The area causing the greatest degree of discomfort usually gets top priority.

A treatment plan should address your most urgent needs first—not necessarily the problems your therapist thinks are most important. Plans that address problems you're not ready to deal with are ineffective, and they give you the sense that your therapist doesn't understand you. In a situation like this, you may end up terminating therapy before you achieve what you set out to do.

A good treatment plan provides direction, teaches new skills, and allows you to experiment in a safe environment.

To return to our previous example, David agreed that his anger was giving him the most trouble. At the very least, it had something to do with his wife's decision to leave. His primary goal, then, was to learn to manage his anger. But anger management means different things to different people. David's challenge was to decide what it meant to him.

Therapist: So, of the goals we've talked about, you feel that learning to manage your anger is the most important for now.

David: Yeah.

Therapist: How will you know when you've become a better manager of your anger?

David: I'm not sure, I guess. Maybe when I'm not so loud. Or when I don't throw things.

Therapist: So what will you be doing instead?

David: I don't know, I really don't know. Leave the room maybe. . . . What do other people do when they get mad?

Therapist: That's a good question. People who grew up in families with domestic violence sometimes learn harmful ways of handling anger and conflict. So here's a little homework assignment. One of the things I'd like you to do between now and the next time we get together is to observe anger in other people—watch their style of anger. What do they do when they get angry? Is what they do the same or different from what you do? Observe people at work, on TV, in the movies. Look for as many examples of anger as you can. Then decide which style of anger you like best, and why. You might even want to jot down a few notes about anger, and when you come in next week, we can go over the research you've gathered.

David: Okay.

David's therapist had started a treatment plan. He divided the plan into four steps: observation, identification, experimenting with change, and evaluation.

Observation

The therapist asked David to observe anger in others for a number of reasons.

• To make David aware of the many different ways people can express anger
   • To help him see alternatives to violent outbursts
   • To have him observe situations that trigger anger in others.
   • To have him witness the effects of anger on others

Observing the behavior of other people is an excellent way to participate in your own treatment. It is risk free, simple to report back on, and requires little in the way of time commitment. Observation is a good springboard for introspection, comparison, and the gathering of additional information about your problem.

Identification

After David observed how other people express anger, the therapist asked him to describe his own anger when something caused him to explode.

At first, David said his explosions came from out of the blue. After further discussion, however, it became apparent to both of them that certain cues could tip David off to an impending blowup. If he could learn to pay attention to the cues, he could choose how to express his anger. This would help keep him from going over the edge.

Some of these cues were internal, some were external. Internally, his chest became tight, his jaws clenched, and he had a rushing feeling that started in his abdomen and traveled up to his throat. He likened this to a flash fire that ignited quickly and spread uncontrollably.

The external cues related to situations that were out of his control. Although his tirades were not as bad at work, he knew that he sometimes flew off the handle when things didn't go his way. Employees who refused to work overtime and go the extra mile, for example, irked him. If he didn't get what he wanted, when he wanted it, he'd simply blow up.

David's explosions had increased over time. Where before they had occurred no more than once a month, now they were happening weekly—and they were getting worse.

Experimentation

Once David could recognize the cues leading up to an explosion, he and his therapist brainstormed about things he could do *instead* of blowing up.

For example, the therapist taught David relaxation techniques to use every time he felt physical anger cues closing in on him. David practiced these techniques every night so he'd be ready to use them at a moment's notice.

Another strategy was to investigate the way David perceived the events that provoked him. Could he be misinterpreting these events? How could he change his perceptions and reduce the potential for an angry response?

Evaluation

Both David and his therapist wanted to know how well these strategies would work. Would his explosions occur less frequently? Would they be less intense? Throughout the treatment, the therapist had David track the frequency and intensity of his outbursts by recording them in a small notebook. For every explosion, David wrote down the time and date. He then rated the severity of each explosion on a scale from 1 to 10. If his outbursts became less frequent or less intense, then his strategies were working. If there was no change, then he and his therapist would have to look more closely at specific events, think of new strategies to change his behavior, and chart his progress again.

There are a number of ways to change your thoughts, feelings, and behaviors. Not every strategy works. Some are exquisite failures. But even failures can bring new information and direction.

Strategies for changing behavior are the result of teamwork between a competent therapist and a willing patient. Knowing where you're going and how to get there makes all the difference.

NOTES

1. Norman Winegar, *The Clinicians Guide to Managed Mental Health Care,* (New York: Haworth Press, 1992).

CHAPTER SEVEN

THE ROLE OF THE THERAPIST

Many years ago, my husband began working for a large insurance company. It was toward the end of the year, and the company invited us to their annual holiday party.

The afternoon of the party, Dennis, one of my husband's colleagues, asked him if we were going to attend and what time we planned to arrive. Then, out of the blue, he said, "Isn't it weird being married to a psychologist? I mean, doesn't she sit around and analyze you all day?"

My husband laughed. Dennis pressed on, "Well, *isn't it?*"

Dennis ventured the question a lot of people would like to ask. It reflects a curiosity about people who sit around listening to other people's problems. It is also based on misperceptions about who mental health professionals are and what we do.

Some of these misperceptions are fed by movies, books, and television. But some can be blamed on the profession itself. The mental health industry prides itself on delivering services without bothering to explain them to clients. Withholding information feeds the "mystery" of therapy, reinforcing the stigma attached to those who are undergoing treatment.

Hopefully, as insurance companies demand better communication, and clients become more assertive about obtaining information, some of these misperceptions will disappear.

This chapter highlights the basic responsibilities of the therapist. The more information you have about the complex role of the therapist, the more confident you will feel in selecting behavioral health services.

THERAPIST AS SELF-MONITOR

Besides focusing on patient care, therapists must monitor their own mental health. Like everyone else, therapists are a product of their personal experiences. The thoughts, feelings, beliefs, and perceptions that come out of these experiences influence the way that therapists treat their patients.

Everyone has issues to settle, reconcile, accept, or understand. A good therapist keeps his or her own psychological house in order. Otherwise, the therapist might mix up his or her own issues with the client's problems, and the client may receive substandard care.

Some therapists go through therapy as part of their training, others seek therapy on their own. Still others consult with a colleague or supervisor when personal issues begin to interfere with their practice.

Self-monitoring is an ongoing procedure. Therapists must continuously note how new experiences influence their thoughts, feelings, and behaviors, and how these, in turn, effect the treatment of their clients.

Like everyone else, therapists have their own set of values that influence how they live and work. It is important that therapists know what their values are. When a therapist encounters a patient with a very different set of values, the therapist must be able to determine if he or she can treat that patient effectively.

Let's say your therapist is a recovering alcoholic—he firmly believes that alcohol is a vice and no one should drink on a regular basis. He feels quite strongly about this. Like most therapists, he asks you about your drinking and drug habits during the assessment.

Let's also say that you drink—rarely to excess, but you enjoy a beer or a glass of wine a couple of times a week. You do not think you have a problem. Your friends and family members have never indicated any concern. You can count on one hand the number of times you've been drunk in the past five years. You've never been picked up for drunk driving, you've never missed work because of a hangover, and you have no legal problems stemming from your use. Your drinking is clearly not a concern to you or anyone else.

Nevertheless, your therapist revisits the topic nearly every session. You start to get the feeling that he thinks you're lying. He implies that you may be minimizing or denying your real pattern of use. You feel irritated, but you're unsure of what to say or do.

If the therapist monitored himself, he would recognize that his own history with alcohol was perhaps skewing his perception about your use. In a case like this, tenacious and misguided questioning may reduce your confidence in the therapist's abilities. If you feel like the therapist missed the boat, you are likely to leave therapy prematurely—and with a negative impression of the process.

Another example: You are a professional woman in your mid-thirties, divorced and dating a never-been-married college professor. The two of you have been seeing each other for six months, and you are head-over-heels in love with him. You want to marry him. He tells you he loves you, but he's not ready to make the big leap. You are angry—furious, actually—and interpret many of his behaviors as signs of rejection. For example, when he goes out with his college professor buddies instead of taking you to a movie, you feel rage—so much rage that you do things to hurt yourself. Sometimes you scratch on your arms and legs with a razor blade until you draw blood, or you pound your fist on the wall until your hand is bruised. Your pattern of self-inflicted injury is not new. In fact, you can remember the first time you cut yourself intentionally—it was in high school after you found out that your boyfriend had been dating one of your friends behind your back.

Your therapist believes that all women who engage in self-injurious behavior were childhood victims of sexual abuse. This is not an outrageous assumption—many women who hurt themselves were, in fact, abuse victims.

You, however, don't remember ever having been sexually abused. You remember other unpleasant aspects of your childhood. Your father was verbally abusive—he called you names, put you down, taunted and ridiculed you mercilessly. You remember how his tirades embarrassed you in front of your friends, so after awhile you stopped bringing friends home. Your mother worked the second shift, so she wasn't around much to see what went on. You tried to tell her, but she was usually too tired to listen. There was nowhere you could go for protection. You felt trapped.

As much as you hated your father, you don't ever remember him being sexual with you. Nor do you recall ever being sexually abused or molested by anyone else.

Your therapist believes that you don't remember. But she doesn't believe you weren't abused. She makes it her mission to uncover what she believes are painful, repressed memories. She recommends a series of exercises, including hypnosis, designed to unlock the secrets she believes you've repressed.

You are skeptical, at best. What you really want to do is figure out how to hang on to the college professor, and maybe learn better ways of handling your anger than cutting and bruising yourself.

The problem in this case is not the therapist's hypothesis, it's what she does with it. By insisting that treatment focus on the recovery of repressed memories, the therapist places her own curiosity, needs, and goals above yours. Her single-minded explanation for your current behavior, combined with a refusal to address the issues you think are important, are a recipe for disaster. One of three things is likely to happen:

• You will terminate treatment prematurely, feeling discouraged from getting real help in the future.

• You will continue with this therapist but feel frustrated and dissatisfied with the treatment.

• You will start to "remember" events that never happened.

The third scenario is especially damaging. If your therapist convinces you something happened when it did not, she has clearly abused her position of power. Furthermore, your own judgment has been undermined by the very person who is supposed to help restore it. Finally, relationships in your family could be destroyed if you assert false accusations.

It is not the therapist's job to unearth what he or she thinks is the truth. A therapist is supposed to focus on what *you* think is true, and address the problems you wish to address. A therapist who knows the importance of self-monitoring understands that his or her needs and curiosity must never supersede the needs of the client.

THERAPIST AS SELF-EVALUATOR

Aside from monitoring their own mental health, good therapists evaluate their strengths and limitations so they can provide the best treatment for their patients.

Who Treats What?

Not all therapists treat all conditions. In fact, very few do. Therapists who claim to treat everything should be regarded with caution, if not with outright skepticism.

Most therapists develop special interests and skills in certain areas. Even therapists who practice as generalists prefer treating some conditions over others. And most therapists have at least one or two areas they don't treat at all, because they aren't interested, haven't been properly trained, or just don't like to.

If your presenting problem is a common one, the majority of therapists will be able to treat it. For example, depression and anxiety are the mental health equivalents of the flu and common cold—both are treated by most clinicians. Trichotillomania (compulsive hair pulling), on the other hand, is a disorder that occurs so infrequently that a therapist could practice for years without ever seeing a case of it.

The following is a list of disorders, common and not so common. If you are seeking help for a less common problem, make sure you select a therapist who has experience treating your disorder.

Common Mental Health Problems

Depressive Disorders
Anxiety Disorders
Adjustment Disorders
Personality Disorders
Alcohol and Drug Dependence
Parent-Child Problems
Marital Problems
Phobias
Post-Traumatic Stress Disorder

Less Common Mental Health Problems

Anorexia
Bulimia
Obsessive-Compulsive Disorder
Pedophilia
Sexual Sadism and Masochism
Kleptomania (Stealing)
Pyromania (Fire setting)
Pathologic Gambling
Trichotillomania (Hair pulling)
Dissociative Identity Disorder (formerly known as Multiple
Personality Disorder)
Schizophrenia

It is common for mental health problems to overlap. Depressed patients, for example, are often anxious as well, and individuals with a personality disorder may also suffer from an eating disorder. Patients who have multiple problems are more difficult to treat. Therefore, therapists must understand their own limits well enough to know which patients they are qualified to work with. Therapists who are unaware of their limits may end up treating (or mistreating) conditions they haven't been trained to handle.

How Many Is Too Many?

When therapists evaluate themselves, they consider how many clients they can see in a day, a week, or a month, and still treat patients effectively. The numbers vary according to the individual and his or her field of training.

For instance, psychiatrists and nurses tend to see more patients per day than nonmedical therapists. This is because most of their patients are simply following up with medication checks and need only fifteen to thirty minutes per session.

Other mental health clinicians usually spend an hour with their patients, so they see fewer clients. For some therapists, four patients a day is plenty. Others may not go above six or eight. Some might see as many as ten a day, but it is hard to imagine how a nonmedical therapist who sees forty or fifty individual patients a week could be effective.

The number of patients a mental health clinician can comfortably see on any given day depends entirely on the therapist's personality, style, energy, and preference.

THERAPIST AS STUDENT

Aside from monitoring their mental health and knowing their strengths and limits, the competent therapist is committed to keeping up with changes in the industry.

Clinical Education

Clinical education for the therapist is a lifelong process that benefits both patient and clinician. A good therapist, like a good student, is curious about human behavior and remains open to new theories and methods of treatment.

Most therapists attend seminars and workshops in their areas of interest and expertise. Licensed therapists are required to complete a certain number of Continuing Education Credits every year or two, depending on state regulations. Clinical education might also include reading or writing books or journal articles, viewing or producing training tapes, and belonging to professional societies.

The Business of the Business

Besides keeping up with clinical advances, therapists must also stay on top of the ever shifting policies of coverage and reimbursement.

Some therapists find business responsibilities difficult, tedious, and cumbersome. "I went to school to be a clinician, not a business person!" is a common complaint. But the complex terrain of health care is demanding more and more attention from the provider.

Good providers will do what they can to keep up with changes in the insurance industry. Some attend insurance or managed care workshops, others read publications or attend seminars to learn about coverage and reimbursement.

CLINICAL RESPONSIBILITIES

The competent therapist assumes a number of responsibilities related to the quality of a patient's care.

Establishing the Relationship

The therapist's first responsibility is to establish a relationship with the patient—a "connection" that invites trust, respect, and ultimately disclosure. A therapist makes this connection by letting you know that he or she is interested in what you are saying. If your therapist listens to you, makes eye contact, and speaks in an agreeable tone of voice, you may feel more comfortable discussing personal issues.

If your therapist avoids eye contact, frequently checks his or her watch, or appears preoccupied with something other than your story, the therapist is forging a bad connection. Inattentive behavior might also include rushing you through your story, finishing your sentences, or falling asleep. If your therapist behaves in this way, it may be time to look for a new therapist.

The length of time it takes to establish a healthy connection depends on the therapist's skill and the patient's history. Some patients have no problem establishing an adequate level of trust. Others, especially those who have been betrayed by authority figures in the past (particularly through physical, sexual, or emotional abuse), may take a much longer time to establish an acceptable level of confidence in the therapist.

Discussing the Diagnosis

The therapist's next responsibility is to make sure that you fully understand the nature of the diagnosis. It is not sufficient to say that you have a major depressive disorder, for example, without explaining what that diagnosis means, outlining your symptoms, and discussing your options for treatment.

A somewhat controversial area of diagnosis involves personality disorders. A personality disorder is an "enduring pattern of inner experience and behavior that deviates markedly from the expectations of the individual's culture, is stable over time, and leads to distress or impairment."[1] Some individuals who suffer from a personality disorder sense that the way they respond to life events is different from those around them, but they don't know why.

Many therapists will choose not to inform a patient that he or she has a personality disorder. Some are uncomfortable discussing personality disorders with their patients. Others feel that patients simply don't need to know—either it's irrelevant to the treatment of other clinical conditions (such as depression or anxiety), or there is little to be done about the personality problem anyway, at least in the short run.

Regardless of a clinician's beliefs, it is his or her responsibility to share the entire diagnosis with you (unless the therapist believes the information would be highly detrimental to your treatment). If you have been diagnosed with a personality disorder, it is generally your right to know. The presence of a personality disorder can have a tremendous influence on the process and outcome of therapy. If you have any questions about your diagnosis, or if you think your therapist is withholding information, ask. It is the therapist's responsibility to give you an honest answer.

Facilitate Problem Solving

Once you understand the diagnosis, the therapist's next job is to help you decide what you want to do about the problem. He or she will help you identify what you want to change, why you want to change it, and how you might go about doing so.

Prioritize

It is likely that you will want to address more than one problem in therapy. Some people that feel there are so many problems they don't know where to begin. The job of the therapist is to help you sort out your concerns so you can put them in order of importance. Although he or she will make suggestions to help you define your priorities, you decide what problems you want to tackle first.

Focus

Your therapist will help you stay focused on your treatment goals by reviewing the previous session, asking about events that occurred between sessions, and following up on homework assignments that may have been given.

Review

As you tackle the most important problems on your list, it is not uncommon for related problems to be resolved along the way. This is why it is important for you and your therapist to periodically review your goals.

Let's say that in the past few months you have become so anxious that you can no longer drive. Your top priority is to reduce your anxiety so you can resume driving. A second goal is to reduce the number of arguments you have with your spouse.

As you reduce your fear of driving and increase your mobility, you notice that you and your spouse are arguing less. You realize that many of your arguments came from your partner's frustration at having to be the primary chauffeur and errand-runner. By managing your first problem, you were able to significantly reduce the second. The therapist's job is to help you understand how your problems are related.

Communicate with Other Providers

If you are seeing a doctor for an ongoing medical condition, tell your therapist. With your permission, the therapist will request information on your medical condition and inform your physician that you are also being treated for emotional problems. This exchange of information is important, because medical problems will sometimes affect emotional problems, and vice versa (see page 91). Problem-solving strategies work best when all of your providers are aware of each other.

Evaluate Progress

Your therapist is responsible for helping you evaluate your progress. Some therapists will review a patient's progress after five or six sessions, others will make an evaluation at the end of every session. Typically, therapists will share these evaluations with their patients.

An evaluation can be as simple as asking clients how they think they are progressing with their goals, then reviewing each goal to determine what still needs to be accomplished.

Other evaluations are more formal. Therapists might have patients complete surveys designed to measure change over time. For instance, the Beck Depression Inventory (BDI) determines whether a patient's symptoms of depression have diminished.

Because this survey is easy to administer, some therapists will use it at the end of every session.

The outcome of an evaluation is used to determine the direction of future treatment. If patients feel they have accomplished most of the goals on their list, they might choose to terminate therapy. If they continue to receive a high score on the BDI after several weeks of treatment, which would indicate significant depression, they might be persuaded to see a psychiatrist for medication.

Confidentiality

Your therapist is responsible for keeping your clinical record confidential. No one can see this information without your written permission. The only exceptions fall under *(a)* mandatory reporting laws (in the suspected abuse of a child or vulnerable adult, or when overt threats are made to harm another individual), and *(b)* requests by a legal authority (in the case of a court order, for example).

If you ask to see your records, your therapist is obligated to give you a copy or show you the original. There may be a nominal charge, but copies must be delivered in a timely fashion.

The only time a therapist may withhold a record is when he or she believes the information would be detrimental to the overall mental health of the client. Situations like these are rare, and most clients who ask to see their records are permitted to do so. Remember, records cannot be released to anyone—not even yourself—without written permission. You will most likely sign a release form to document that the record was, in fact, released.

THE BUSINESS RESPONSIBILITIES

In addition to their clinical responsibilities, providers attend to a number of business obligations. Many of these won't have an immediate or direct effect on what happens during a therapy session, but a therapist's failure to comply with good business practices could have disastrous effects down the road.

Some business responsibilities are essential. These are either governed by licensing boards or considered standards of practice by leaders in the industry. Other responsibilities are discretionary—the therapist can choose whether or not to practice them.

Essential Responsibilities

Accurate Representation

Mental health providers must represent themselves accurately in both verbal and written materials. Degrees must be listed on business cards, and licenses must be displayed in the therapist's office. Clinicians may not practice outside of their areas of expertise.

License

Providers need to keep their license up-to-date. They must pay a renewal fee to the licensing board and complete a certain number of Continuing Education Credits every year.

Explanation of Insurance Participation

In an ideal world, all therapists would cooperate with all insurance companies to obtain the maximum financial benefits for their patients. In reality, however, many therapists don't like dealing with insurance companies, so they don't. This is not unethical, as long as they make their position clear from the beginning. If a therapist is unwilling to participate in insurance reviews, he or she should explain how this will affect reimbursement.

Therapists who refuse to work with insurance companies are responsible for telling you so before the end of your first session. In this case, you will have to complete the insurance reimbursement forms, or pay for the sessions, yourself.

Cannot Abandon Care

A therapist cannot stop seeing a patient without first arranging treatment with another provider. This would be considered an abandonment of care.

Let's say you have been seeing Dr. Smith for depression. Four months into your treatment, your employer changes insurance companies. Dr. Smith is not on the new insurance company's provider list. You cannot afford to pay Dr. Smith yourself, so you need to find a new therapist. It is Dr. Smith's responsibility to refer you to another provider.

Availability

Therapists are expected to be available for emergencies twenty-four hours a day, or they must arrange for another therapist to cover for them. Many therapists direct their patients to call the local hospital or crisis center if they have an emergency after hours. Others participate in an on-call group, so if you have an emergency after regular business hours, you can phone your therapist's office. An answering service will either connect you with an on-call provider or take your name and number and have the provider return your call.

Twenty-four-hour services are for emergencies only. Do not call if your problem can wait until the next business day.

Record Keeping

Therapists are supposed to keep records, but not all of them do. Clinical records have been the subject of numerous debates and professional workshops. The increasingly litigious atmosphere in which professionals practice has many clinicians wondering what information, and how much, they should keep on file.

Some therapists believe that the less said in clinical records, the less chance there is for misinterpretation. Others feel just the opposite—the more said, the better protected they will be against a lawsuit.

Many therapists take a common sense approach and include the basics: patient history, symptoms, test results, diagnosis, treatment goals, treatment plans, and medications. Phone calls to and from other providers are usually documented as well.

Aside from the legal implications, one of the strongest arguments for keeping good records is to ensure continuity of care. For example, if your therapist were to win the lottery tomorrow and quit practice, a complete clinical record would help the next provider know what you were working on. If you lose your therapist for any reason, a good clinical record means you won't have to start all over again.

Clinical records also establish a context for each episode of care. If you were in therapy several months ago and decided to seek help again, a good clinical record would trace your progress during previous episodes.

Diagnosis and Payment

Your therapist is not only responsible for diagnosing and treating your condition, he or she must also report your diagnosis to your insurance company. Most companies will pay for some diagnoses but not for others. If your condition is not covered, you will be responsible for payment.

Some therapists play the diagnosis game—they treat you for a condition that is not covered under your plan, but when they submit the bill to the insurance company, they name a different diagnosis, one that *is* covered under your plan. This is not only unethical, it is also considered fraudulent.

Fee Maximums and Networks

Managed care plans use network providers who agree to provide services for a set, reduced fee. Beware of the therapist who attempts to bill you for the difference between the contracted rate and his or her usual fee.

Let's say the therapist's regular fee is $125 per hour. As a network provider, however, the therapist agrees to charge the plan's discount rate of $80 per hour, which includes a $20 co-payment. You pay the therapist $20 and your insurance pays the remaining $60. The therapist may not bill you for the $45 difference. Charging you more than your co-payment would constitute a violation of his or her contract with the managed care company. If the therapist attempts to bill you for the difference, you should refuse to pay—and let your plan know immediately.

Discretionary Practices

In addition to the essential business responsibilities, some therapists follow voluntary business practices that allow patients to obtain therapy more easily. Whether or not to follow these practices is entirely up to the clinician.

Punctuality

Therapy sessions should start within a few minutes of the scheduled time. Some therapists, however, seem to run fifteen to twenty minutes late for each appointment. This can be a problem, especially if you have taken off work in the middle of the day, hired a baby sitter, or have another appointment you need to keep. Your time is valuable, and your therapist should respect this. If he or she is consistently late for appointments, the two of you need to discuss it.

Occasionally, a crisis situation may cause your therapist to be late for an appointment, just as an emergency may delay you on occasion. The therapist should explain the delay, but you can still expect a full therapy session. In rare instances, a crisis may cause the therapist to cancel your appointment entirely. If this happens, you should be able to reschedule quickly.

Availability

If you and your therapist agree to meet every two weeks, the therapist should be able to keep to this schedule. If you frequently find yourself waiting longer than the agreed upon interval, ask the therapist if he or she can accommodate you. Many therapists do not schedule their own appointments and may not be aware of the problem. If your therapist cannot oblige you, you may want to ask for a referral to a therapist who can.

Interruptions

Most therapists prohibit telephone calls, pagers, and other interruptions during therapy sessions. Some clinicians have support staff or an answering service to intercept calls. If the therapist is on-call, however, he or she may need to respond to a crisis promptly. On-call providers will generally inform their patients of their on-call status. If your therapist is called out of your session, he or she should make arrangements to continue or reschedule as soon as possible.

Community Resources

Community-based resources can be a tremendous help to patients in therapy. Many of these resources are support groups run by members of the community. A knowledgeable therapist is aware of the different resources in the community and can refer patients as needed. For example:

• A man who recently lost his wife of twenty-five years might find comfort in a group for widowers.

• A couple seeking therapy to deal with the disruptive behavior of their six-year-old son may benefit from a parenting group.

• Parents with children suffering from attention deficit disorder (ADD) can join support groups for parents with ADD children.

• A woman recently diagnosed with breast cancer may find comfort in a breast cancer support group.

• A young woman who has struggled with her sexual orientation might find help "coming out" in a group for lesbians.

THE THERAPEUTIC RELATIONSHIP

The relationship between a client and therapist is a professional one, which implies that there are certain limits on personal interactions. In order to create a comfortable working relationship, the therapist must demonstrate a genuine interest in the client's problem, while maintaining a personal distance. Sometimes it's a difficult line to walk.

Safety

A client should feel safe enough to explore personal concerns under the guidance of a well-trained and competent clinician without fear of abuse. It is the therapist's job to ensure this safety.

Therapists establish boundaries to provide a safe environment for the client. A boundary is an imaginary line that separates the therapist's personal business from yours.

Your personal problems are the therapist's business. That's why you came to therapy in the first place. The therapist's personal problems, however, are not your concern. He or she should not bring them up, or even allude to them, during a session. Therapists are expected to keep a check on their own issues so they don't become a part of your therapy.

No matter how well intended, crossing the boundary is inappropriate and potentially exploitive. As the consumer, you must be able to recognize such an infraction if it were to occur.

Friendship

Therapists are not friends. They are not peers. They are professionals you pay to provide a specific service related to your mental health needs.

A therapist should never approach a client as a friend or potential member of a social network. This means the therapist does not talk about things that are usually associated with more intimate relationships, such as his or her spouse, partner, children, work, and so forth.

A therapist should never invite you to participate in social engagements. While it is acceptable for your therapist to suggest an increase in your social activity, it should be with members of your own social network—never with the therapist.

Your therapist is crossing social boundaries if he or she:

• Talks at length about family members or discusses family outings, activities, vacations, and so forth

• Asks your opinion on any of the above

• Leads you to believe that a relationship outside of the therapeutic relationship is possible, for example, if the therapist invites you to dinner, coffee, or an activity in which you share a mutual interest (such as art shows, sporting events, or the theater)

• Invites you to a family function, like a wedding, birthday party, christening, or bar or bas mitzvah

• Offers to set you up on a blind date with a friend

Dual Relationships

Therapists may not make requests that would form any type of "dual relationship." This means if you are engaged in a business of interest to the therapist, he or she may not ask advice, solicit deals, or trade therapy services for any other service.

If you are a stockbroker, for example, it is improper for the therapist to purchase stocks through you or ask for investment advice. The same holds true if you are an attorney, physician, car mechanic, car dealer, caterer, jeweler, dentist, grocer, or any other type of profession.

Sexual Relationships

It is not at all unusual for patients to have sexual feelings for their therapist. It is up to the therapist, however, to help clarify those feelings and refrain from encouraging sexual feelings and fantasies. The therapist also needs to make it clear that an intimate relationship with the patient is not possible.

Occasionally, therapists will experience sexual feelings for a client, but competent therapists will not discuss these feelings with the client. Instead, he or she will seek consultation from a supervisor in order to deal with these feelings without jeopardizing the patient's care.

There are times—not many, but it does happen—when a therapist's judgment is so impaired that he or she engages in an intimate relationship with a patient. When this happens, the therapist transgresses all sorts of boundaries: emotional, psychological, physical, and sexual. This is considered abusive.

The transgression of sexual boundaries is not limited to sexual intercourse. In many cases, intercourse may not actually occur. When it does, it is merely the culmination of a number of other transgressions that constitute abuse.

Be alert if your therapist does any of the following:

• Offers to meet you outside therapy sessions for coffee, dinner, or any other social activity

• Sets up regularly scheduled appointments at places other than the office, such as a bar, restaurant, hotel, and so forth

• Persistently comments on your appearance or clothing

• Engages in sexual questioning that seems excessive or unrelated to your presenting problem

• Offers to see you anytime, anywhere

• Gives you hugs or touches you in ways that make you feel uncomfortable

• Lets you know that he or she is interested in dating you

• Offers to terminate therapy so you can start seeing each other socially

Boundary transgressions are always confusing for patients. Sexual transgressions are particularly egregious, because healthy sexual interactions can only occur in relationships where the power is balanced to begin with.

Power is never balanced in a client-therapist relationship—the client is always the vulnerable party. When a therapist initiates or responds to sexual contact, or suggests that a sexual relationship is possible, it is considered a gross breach of trust, responsibility, and ethics.

Reporting Trouble

If you are concerned about your therapist's behavior, you should report it.

If the behavior is related to a style issue, such as chronic tardiness or the refusal to answer nonemergency phone calls, you might want to talk with the therapist first. If this doesn't help, or you are simply too uncomfortable to discuss it face-to-face, file a complaint with the therapist's supervisor. The supervisor will review the complaint, most likely speak with the therapist, then get back to you to let you know that the problem has been addressed.

If there has been a boundary transgression, you may file a complaint with the supervisor or go directly to the board that issued the therapist's license.

Many clients are concerned about reporting a complaint because they don't want to get their therapist in trouble. This is especially true when boundaries have been crossed. It is often difficult for patients to report boundary transgressions, because they feel like they are betraying the therapist's trust and the specialness of the relationship.

In some cases, therapists tell patients not to reveal details of their relationship so they won't get in trouble. If you are in a situation like this and feel unable or unwilling to make a formal report, get a second opinion from another therapist. He or she will file the report for you, since therapists are obligated to report cases of suspected patient abuse to the licensing board.

NOTES

1. Michael B. First, MD, ed., *Diagnostic and Statistical Manual of Mental Disorders, Fourth Edition,* (Washington, D.C.: American Psychological Association, 1994), 629.

CHAPTER EIGHT

THE ROLE OF THE CLIENT

Most mental health professionals don't discuss the role of the client. They don't believe that teaching someone how to be a client is part of their job. And most clients don't ask, because they're not quite sure where to start.

When questions go unanswered, clients end up feeling disgruntled and dissatisfied. Predictably, clients who are not quite sure of their role are likely to leave therapy before accomplishing their goals. But it doesn't have to be like that.

The role of the client is not confusing or elusive; in fact, it is similar to the role of the therapist. An effective client, like a competent therapist, has three primary areas of responsibility: self-monitor, self-evaluator, and student. Understanding your responsibilities will go a long way toward helping you get the most out of therapy.

Client as Self-Monitor

Whether we know it or not, most of us are aware of how we react to events in our lives. For example, statements like "That really makes me sad" or "I was so disappointed" indicate that we are paying emotional attention to ourselves. This monitoring is important because it influences the decisions we make, especially as we confront major, often unsettling, life events. Take the following scenarios, for example:

• Naomi finds out that her husband of ten years fathered a child before he met her.

• Sam, an engineer hopeful, receives a rejection letter from the graduate program he was determined to attend.

• Jason wrestles with his mother's decision to place his father in a nursing home.

• Laurie decides she is sick and tired of her boyfriend's chronic lying and moves out of their apartment.

Each of these events is destined to upset life's balance. But not everyone responds to significant events in the same way. One person may be preoccupied, driven to excessive and meaningless tasks; another may have a hard time simply getting out of bed.

Sustaining a major hit and getting knocked off balance is not all bad. It may be painful, but it opens up an opportunity to inventory other critical areas of our lives. Goals, accomplishments, wishes, hopes, dreams, and psychological well-being all come under scrutiny. It's like a bucket of cold water—if nothing else, it gets our attention.

When we pay attention to how we react in different situations, we are in a much better position to know when we are doing well and when we are not. This plays a significant role in the decision to make that first call to the therapist's office.

What's Wrong?

Before you come in for your first session, ask yourself, "What's wrong?" Most often, the response to this question is the event that triggered our distress.

Describing the event is a good place to start, but it's not enough. Different individuals will react differently to the same event, so it is important to describe your response. For example, Jason reacted with anger and disappointment when his mother placed his father in a nursing home. Another person in that situation might have been relieved, since his mother would no longer have to bear the increasingly difficult responsibility of caring for an infirm spouse.

Do not assume that the therapist will automatically know what you are thinking or feeling. Describe your reaction, and be as explicit as you can. For many clients, this is easier said than done.

Make a List

Start by purchasing a small notebook to carry around with you during your treatment. Before you come in for your first session, think about what is wrong and write down your concerns and issues. Don't worry about organizing the material, just get it down on paper. Once you feel your list is complete, read it over a couple of times to yourself. Then read it out loud. Hearing yourself speak clearly about your concerns is a personal admission—it means you recognize that something is wrong and you intend to do something about it.

Your notebook will also come in handy if you want to jot down ideas, take notes during sessions, keep track of homework assignments, or chart your progress.

The following are the lists kept by the four people mentioned earlier. Notice how each of these individuals separated the event from the effects of the event. It will be helpful to both you and your therapist if you make this distinction as well.

Naomi's List

Situation

I just found out that my husband fathered a child with an old girlfriend before we were married.

Reaction

• I'm shocked that he didn't tell me before we were married.

• I can't sleep and I feel jumpy, especially every time the phone rings. I keep expecting to hear from the child's mother or a lawyer or somebody.

• I'm mad at him and irritable with the kids.

• I don't want to have sex with him anymore.

• I wonder what else I don't know about him.

Sam's List

Situation

I was rejected by the graduate school I wanted to attend, and I don't know what to do.

Reaction

• I feel hopeless.

• I'm a failure.

• I don't have a clue about what I'm going to do now.

• I'm jealous of my friends who got in, and I can't stand to hang around them anymore.

Jason's List

Situation

My mother has decided to put my father in a nursing home, and I think she's making the wrong decision.

Reaction

• I get physically sick every time I think about my dad having to go to one of those places.
• Nobody will listen to my suggestions that could help keep him at home.
• I'm sad all the time.
• My wife and I argue over the dumbest things lately.
• Things are tense with my brothers and sisters.

Laurie's List

Situation

I left my boyfriend because he's been lying to me since the day we met.

Reaction

• Since I left, I've been living on my own and I hate it.
• How do I know I made the right decision?
• I always seem to end up with jerks for boyfriends and I'm tired of it.
• I feel nervous all the time.
• I'm afraid to tell my friends and family that I've left.

What's Right?

Monitoring what's wrong is only part of the task. You also need to ask yourself, "What's right?" To someone in distress, this may seem like an impossible question. Who wants to think about what's right when you're steeped in so much that's wrong?

Like it or not, knowing what's right is essential to problem solving. When we acknowledge our resources, we feel less apprehensive about tackling our problems.

Let's say that one morning, you're padding around the kitchen when you notice your socks are getting wet. You unplugged the kitchen sink just last week, so that's not the culprit. You walk over to the stove and dishwasher, and by this time your socks are soaked. The dishwasher is running but it looks okay. No, wait a minute. Out from under the baseboard you see a visible stream of soapy water seeping across your new hardwood floor.

At this point, you have a number of choices. You could panic and start yelling about the damage your old dishwasher caused to the new floor. You could throw things at the ancient beast, hoping to beat it into submission. You could turn it off and call for help. You could turn if off, get the toolbox, and try to fix it yourself. You could call a neighbor. (If your neighbor is a plumber, then this is truly your lucky day.) You could change your socks, walk away, and do absolutely nothing.

"What's right" includes all of the resources we can call upon for help. Pull out that little notebook again and begin listing your resources. Think of your resources as a psychological toolbox. Everybody has at least a few tools; the trick is to recognize them for what they are. Resources might include the following:

- A good friend
- An understanding boss
- Supportive family members
- Financial stability
- A good lawyer
- A sense of humor
- Persistence
- A church group
- A satisfying hobby

Through self-monitoring, we become aware of how we react to significant events in our lives. We learn to inventory our resources and recognize that when we "hit the wall," feel lost, or don't know what to do, we may we need professional intervention. Finally, self-monitoring prompts us to follow through with therapy.

CLIENT AS SELF-EVALUATOR

The ability to evaluate your progress in therapy is an essential skill. Are you getting what you want out of therapy? Do you feel like you're moving in the right direction?

If not, find out why, because you will need to do something about it. Don't let yourself pretend that it's out of your control.

Clients are likely to feel dissatisfied with therapy if:
- Their expectations aren't being met,
- The therapist and client are a poor match, or
- They are contributing to their own lack of progress.

As the client, your job is to evaluate each of these possibilities and do what you can to resolve the problem.

Expectations

You may feel dissatisfied with therapy because your expectations aren't being met. For example:

- You expected to feel better by now, but don't.
- Your therapist declines to give you an opinion on what you should be doing.
- You feel misunderstood, like your therapist can't relate to what you're feeling.
- Homework assignments don't make sense.
- Your therapist provides little feedback or direction.
- Your therapist is booked all the time so it's hard to get a return appointment.
- Therapy is too expensive.
- Your therapist is regularly late for appointments.
- Your therapist frequently reschedules your appointments.

As the client, it is your responsibility to evaluate your expectations and determine whether or not they are realistic.

Let's say you're frustrated because your therapist is frequently fifteen minutes late for your appointments. You expect your therapist to be on time. Is this realistic? Yes. Do you deserve an explanation and an apology? Yes. Is your dissatisfaction justified? Yes. For therapy to be successful, you need to tell your therapist about your concerns and expectations. Otherwise, future sessions may be tainted by your ongoing irritation with the therapist.

Let's take another example. You expected to feel better by now but you don't. Is your expectation realistic? It depends. The rate of improvement is different for each client, but if you've been in therapy for what you think is a long time, and you're not feeling any better (or you're feeling worse), let the therapist know.

Some clients demonstrate their dissatisfaction indirectly. They show up late for appointments, cancel at the last minute, or "forget" about them altogether. They don't finish their homework or they leave assignments at home. Some simply discontinue therapy.

Your therapist is not a mind reader. He or she might surmise from your behavior that something is wrong, but you are not likely to remedy the problem unless you address it.

The most pragmatic approach is to speak directly with your therapist about your concerns. Most therapists welcome comments about the therapy process, even negative ones. Tell your therapist why you're dissatisfied. In the long run, it will be a greater benefit to you than your therapist.

If you can't bring yourself to discuss your concerns in person, write a letter, send an e-mail, or leave a voice-mail message. The point is not how you communicate, but that you take responsibility to do so.

The Therapeutic Team

Therapists are not always well matched to their clients. Poor matches might reflect a difference in values or personalities, and can lead to client dissatisfaction.

For example, your therapist may be too confrontational, docile, or aloof for your personality. You may be uncomfortable with your therapist's beliefs, or he or she may decline to reveal information that you feel is necessary to your treatment (such as the therapist's religion).

If you are concerned that you and your therapist are not a good match, discuss it with the therapist. The two of you can talk it out, and if you are still uncomfortable, he or she can help you find a provider who will be more compatible.

Client Contribution

If you are dissatisfied with therapy, it is possible that your attitude toward treatment could be the culprit. It is essential that you take the time to evaluate yourself. You may be contributing to your own lack of progress, particularly if you do any of the following:

- Say what you think the therapist wants to hear
- Resist the therapist's efforts to help you focus on one issue
- Neglect to reveal information relevant to your treatment
- Refuse to do homework assignments
- Participate in therapy only because someone else is insisting that you get help

If you find yourself in any of these situations, chances are you're not making much progress. Your therapist can help you remedy these issues, if you are willing to talk about them. If you cannot discuss them with your therapist, a friend, or another confidant, and you are not ready to change them on your own, then you need to reconsider therapy at this particular point in time.

CLIENT AS STUDENT

So far we've talked about your responsibilities as self-monitor—knowing what's wrong, what's right, and why you've decided to seek therapy. We've also discussed your role as self-evaluator—examining your expectations, your compatibility with the therapist, and your own contributions toward treatment. An equally important element in the therapy process is your role as a student.

As a psychotherapy client, you are simply a student of your own behavior. The word "behavior," here, describes thoughts and feelings as well as actions. Learning about your own behavior—and learning how to change it—is the primary goal of therapy.

Observe

Your first task as a student is to become aware of the behavior you wish to study. It could be anger, depression, jealousy, anxiety, an eating disorder, or any number of problems that make life difficult.

Observe yourself. How do you know that the problem is a problem? When does it occur, and under what circumstances? How often does it happen? How long has it been going on? How does it affect your day-to-day living? What kind of feedback have you received from the people around you?

Take out that little notebook again and label a page "Observations." When a problem arises, note the time, date, and details. By keeping a record of ongoing occurrences, you may start to see a trend. Share these observations with your therapist and continue recording for your future reference.

Explore

Like any good student, once you identify the behavior you wish to study, start gathering information. Begin with the people around you. What do they think of your problem? Check newspapers and magazines for information. Browse through books at the library. Cruise the Internet. Go to the bookstore. Listen to the conversations around you and make a mental note each time your topic comes up.

It's one thing for your therapist to say that your problem is not uncommon. It's another thing entirely to meet, read about, or hear of other people who are dealing with the same issues. The sense that you are not alone, that there are others who struggle with your same concerns, is called universality.

Universality reduces the sense that you are the only one in the world coping with a particular problem. It helps to know that others have struggled with, and resolved, some of the same issues. It gives you a chance to learn from people who have been down the road before

171

you. What worked for them? What didn't? Are there lessons you can take from their experiences? It is often comforting to know that you are one of a number of people coping with the same problem.

Experiment

No matter how you look at it, moving from where you are to where you want to be will take some experimentation. As a student of behavior, it's essential to take risks and try new perspectives.

Experimentation is like shopping for new clothes. You browse through the different options. Something catches your eye and you wonder if you should try it on. You decide to go for it, so you head off to the changing room and slip into your selection. You evaluate your decision. Does it fit? Do you like it? It is comfortable? Is it you?

Experimentation allows us to try out different behaviors and decide whether or not to keep them. Like trying on new clothes, it is usually an activity that occurs in private. Privacy allows you to review your choices more discreetly. If it fits and you like it, it's yours. If not, you can always put it back and try something else.

Commit

Self-observation, exploration, and experimentation are useless without a commitment to change. As a student, you must promise yourself to follow through with the skills you've acquired. Committing to change is like learning how to type—it takes practice. And not just for a couple of days, but for months, years—maybe even a lifetime.

When it comes to therapy, there are no magic cures. Success depends on hard work and a solid therapeutic relationship. As the client, you play a powerful role in your own treatment. Learn it well.

CLIENT RESPONSIBILITIES

Therapy is not something that is given to you by a mental health clinician. It is a team effort. As part of this team, you, like your therapist, have certain responsibilities to the therapy process.

Motivation

To succeed in therapy, you need to be motivated to work (see chapter 2). There are a number of factors that influence motivation, including emotional pain, disruption in relationships, and legal problems.

Motivation runs on a continuum. The more motivated you are, the more likely you are to succeed in therapy.

Disclosure of Information

What you tell your therapist is up to you, but the more information you share, the more effective your treatment will be.

Some things are easier to talk about than others. You might go on and on about how you're having trouble sleeping at night, but you may feel decidedly reluctant to talk about how your Uncle Al sexually molested you when you were a child. You certainly have the right to refrain from discussing difficult or embarrassing information. But understand that by withholding information, you slow the progress of therapy.

Let's say that Jason's relationship with his father was a violent one. The abuse started when Jason was a young boy, and ended only after he went away to college. Nevertheless, his father always made sure that Jason had enough money. When it was time to go to college, he could choose any university in the country, all expenses paid.

When Jason's therapist asked about his family history, Jason denied having any difficulties with his father. But the relationship clearly affected Jason's reaction to his father going into a nursing home. Continuing to withhold information about this might spare him some embarrassment, but it will also keep him from resolving the issue. In the end, Jason is likely to be disappointed with therapy.

Questions

Ever good student asks questions—it's one of the best ways to educate yourself about the therapy process. Frequently asked questions include:

- How often will we meet?
- How long is each session?
- How many times do I have to come here?
- Have you ever worked with anybody like me before?
- Are there any books I can read that will help me understand what I'm working on?
- Are there any groups in the community that would be helpful?
- How much do the sessions cost?
- What happens if I miss a session?
- Can I bring my (husband, wife, son, daughter) into the sessions with me?

When it comes to personal questions, however, therapists will generally refrain from answering, stating instead that they don't discuss their private lives.

This response can be confusing to patients, who reveal highly sensitive information about themselves. "I'm telling you about me. Why can't I know a little about you?"

You are certainly entitled to professional information about your therapist—degrees, training, competencies, and so forth. Personal information, however, is not relevant to your therapy.

Report Concerns

If you are uncomfortable with your therapist's behavior, report it to the proper authority (see chapter 7).

If you're not sure if your therapist is behaving inappropriately, report it anyway. You are not expected to make that determination—that's the job of the supervisor or licensing board. Your responsibility is to file a report if you suspect wrongdoing.

Some patients choose to inform the therapist that they are filing a complaint. This is not necessary, of course. You may, however, wish to contact the therapist's supervisor if you want help in finding another clinician.

Respect the Therapist's Time

Most therapy appointments run fifty minutes. Many therapists use the ten minutes after the session to document the patient's progress. While it is not your responsibility to watch the clock, it is helpful to pay attention to the therapist's cues toward the end of the session. The therapist might say, "We've only got a couple of minutes left, so let's summarize," or "We need to end in a minute or two."

Unfortunately, some patients wait until the end of the session to bring up their most significant concerns: "Oh, by the way, just wanted to let you know I decided I'm leaving my wife," or "I thought you might need to know that I've just been diagnosed with HIV." Many patients make announcements like these at the end of the session to avoid dealing with the underlying issues.

The point at which you choose to reveal information is your decision, but dropping a bomb at the end of the session is not productive for either you or the therapist (although it's better than not revealing the information at all). Try addressing important issues earlier in the session, so you and your therapist can explore them together.

Keep Appointments

If you cannot keep your appointment, call to cancel as soon as you know you won't be able to make it. This gives you an opportunity to reschedule, and it allows the therapist to schedule another patient in your old time slot.

Some therapists have policies about missed appointments. If you cancel a session less than twenty-four hours before the appointment time, you may have to pay a penalty. If you skip an appointment without calling to cancel, you may have to pay the entire fee. Neither of these scenarios are covered by insurance, so if you are charged for a missed session, the fee is your responsibility.

CHAPTER NINE

PROBLEM SOLVING, PROBLEM MANAGEMENT

We are a "fix-it" society, enamored with the idea that if something is wrong we can make it right. If it hurts, we can block the pain. If it is crooked, we can make it straight. Jagged edges can be rubbed smooth so we can live happily ever after.

We believe that if we do everything right, the things that confuse, plague, or trouble us will somehow disappear.

Sometimes this is true. Often, it is not.

The problem is, in our search for the perfect solution, we neglect to consider what we expect that solution to bring.

SOLUTIONS

Solutions are answers to finite problems. A finite problem is one that has a definite end. Once it is fixed, it needs no further attention.

Math problems are finite. Once they are solved, they stay solved. A dripping faucet, a broken fan belt, and a flat tire are also finite problems. With the right tools and a bit of time, the problem goes away.

Unfortunately, human problems are rarely finite. Even if we manage to "solve" a problem, we might end up with something we hadn't expected.

EXPECTATIONS

Many clients come into therapy looking for The Answer. Wanting to know "why" is one of the most common motives for crossing the therapeutic threshold. "I just want to know why my husband drinks," "Why my daughter and I don't get along," "Why I'm having an affair, " "Why I eat so much."

The problem with "why" is not so much in wanting an answer, it is in failing to recognize what we want the answer to bring. Very simply, we expect that answers to our problems will automatically lead to cures and solutions. "If I knew what was wrong, I could fix the problem and make it go away."

With interpersonal relationships, this is rarely the case. There are no quick fixes when it comes to a relationship with your spouse, partner, child, parent, co-worker, or boss. Rather than give us solutions, answering "why" shows us there is work to be done.

The good news is, even when problems cannot be solved, they can usually be managed. Finding out "why" gives us a chance to develop the skills we need to manage our problems effectively.

David's Anger

Let's revisit the case of David, the computer consultant from chapter 1. Recall that David's wife left him, saying she wouldn't live with his outbursts any longer. After finding her note, David had a fit, threw a few things around the house, and then stomped off to see a therapist.

In therapy, David admitted that he had problems dealing with anger, and not just toward his wife. He had blown up at his employees, too. A couple of them had even quit. Eventually, David was able to identify a pattern: he would get irritated, blow up, and alienate people he cared about. He hadn't been especially concerned about it, though, until Karen left.

David's question was, "Why do I get so mad?"

David fully expected the answer to this question to lead to a simple solution. He thought, "If I knew why I got so mad, I could fix it and not get mad in the future."

To help David find out why he got so mad, the therapist asked him to describe events that made him angry over the past several months. David was able to list quite a few.

I got mad when . . .

- Karen decided to go to medical school.
- I found out she was studying with a male colleague.
- Karen moved out of the house.
- An employee refused to work overtime.
- A client complained about a computer program I'd installed.
- The office furniture I ordered failed to arrive on time.
- The bank made an error on my checking account statement.
- Some guy cut in front of me on the freeway.

David noticed that the situations on this list had one thing in common—they were all out of his control. This was the answer to David's question: "Why do I get so mad? Because some things are out of my control."

Although the answer was enlightening, it did not solve David's problem with anger. There would be many situations he couldn't control. Avoiding these situations was impossible; attempting to do so, unhealthy. "I get mad when I'm not in control. Much of what goes on around me is beyond my control. Does this mean I'll spend the rest of my life blowing up and sending people away?"

To help David with his dilemma, the therapist worked with him to reframe his idea of anger. To David, anger was confusing and destructive. It pushed people away and made him feel bad about himself. He tried to ignore his angry feelings, but they kept bubbling over. Anger seemed to be just another event that he couldn't control.

Over time, the therapist helped David understand that anger was a normal part of life—it could be a useful tool for dealing with his feelings, and it didn't have to alienate the people around him. David's problem was not his anger, it was how he expressed his anger. Once David understood this, he and his therapist could find ways to manage the problem.

Sarah and Jack

Sarah and Jack have been married for fifteen years. They have an eleven-year-old son and a four-year-old daughter. Jack is a buyer for a large retail chain. He spends much of his time traveling, looking at new product lines, and making purchases for stores in his region.

Sarah finished her PhD in chemistry shortly before the birth of their second child. Juggling schoolwork, her dissertation, child care, and a traveling husband was difficult. For the past few years,

Sarah has been working as a researcher for a national drug company. She loves her job but feels overwhelmed much of the time.

Sarah and Jack have been unhappy in their marriage for years. Neither one wants to divorce, but both recognize that the marriage is in trouble. They bicker constantly about little things—cooking, picking up around the house, laundry, grocery shopping. They have occasional blowouts over bigger issues like sex, money, and disciplining the children. The only thing they seem to agree on is that they disagree about almost everything.

The couple finally decided to get help after their son ran away from home, leaving a note saying how much he hated living in the family. He told them not to worry, that he was going somewhere where people didn't hate each other so much. The boy was gone for nearly twenty-four hours before the police picked him up at the local Greyhound station, just as he was about to board a bus to his grandmother's house, three states away. It was a nasty wake-up call, but Sarah phoned the next day for an appointment with a marriage therapist.

They spent their first sessions discussing marital concerns.

Sarah's Story

"I'm mad all the time, and I hate it. There are so many things about Jack that drive me crazy. For one thing, I'm organized and punctual. When we're supposed to be somewhere, I try to get there a few minutes early. Jack thinks it's close enough if we get there within a half an hour of when we're supposed to. We've been late for dinner parties, doctor's appointments, movies, and school conferences for the kids. I think it's irresponsible.

"And I'm tired of doing all the work around the house. Okay, I know he travels. But when he's home I expect him to do his share. When we were first married, we divided up the chores, and it worked for a while. But then he'd 'forget' to do his, or he wouldn't do them very well, and I'd end up taking over. For example, he'd do the laundry, but he'd never read the instructions on the clothes. One time he ruined three of my good silk blouses. Another time, he turned all the white sheets pink because he didn't sort the colors from the whites. I gave up on him and decided to do it myself.

"Then he said he'd take care of the bills. That lasted eight months, until the late notices started piling up. I got mad about having to pay those finance charges for late payments—it's stupid to pay extra. He'd say it was no big deal, but to me, it was money down the drain. The real topper, though, was when we got the shut-off notice from the phone company! I mean, there was no excuse for that. So I started doing the bills.

"Same thing with grocery shopping—money's not a big deal to him. I clip coupons, watch for sales, and buy generic brands. When he goes to the store, he buys all brand names, never looks for specials, and brings home a steak that costs $8 a pound, when a roast costing $3 a pound would have been fine. So guess who's doing the shopping now?

"And, I'm the disciplinarian—I keep the kids in line while he's on the road. I make sure they do their homework, come in on time, and don't watch too much TV. Then he comes home, and it's like Christmas! His arms are full of presents, the kids are ecstatic to see him, and I'm the witch.

"I'm tired of prodding him all the time to do his fair share. When I tell him I'm mad, he sits there and says nothing. Sometimes I think he does some of this stuff on purpose, just to get me mad. It's like I've got three kids instead of two. We hardly do anything together anymore. I just don't feel like he's a partner.

"My question is, why can't he shape up, be a little more responsible? Act like a husband instead of an adolescent? If I knew the answer to that, everything else would be fine."

Jack's Story

"She's right about one thing, I hate fighting. I think it's pointless. But things aren't exactly the way she says they are.

"Okay, I admit it's not nearly as important for me to be on time as it is for her—I just don't get what the big deal is. She always has to be the very first one to arrive wherever we're going, so we're usually ten to twenty minutes early. It's a waste of time, sitting around waiting for something to start. People are usually late anyway, so we sit around even longer—waiting—and I hate to wait.

"Another problem is that I don't think Sarah has any idea how hard it is to travel. When I first started, I really hated being on the road. I missed her and the kids, and I still feel guilty about not seeing them when I'm away. That's why I come home with presents. I know it doesn't make up for my not being there, but it makes me feel a little better, and it lets them know I was thinking about them.

"As for the bills, I was only late a handful of times in the eight months that I did them. And the shut-off notice for the phone happened because the bill got stuck under the drawer and I didn't see it for three months.

"When Sarah wants something done, she wants it done *now.* When I come home from a trip, the last thing I want to do is write out a stack of bills or go to the grocery store. It's not that I'm unwilling, it's just that I need a little downtime first—a chance to say 'hi', find out what's going on, talk, and hang out for a while. Relax. Sarah doesn't know the meaning of the word 'relax.' It's always go, go, go. I don't see what's so offensive about taking a nap, reading the paper, or just sitting down for a bit.

"It's so hectic and tense at home that I actually look forward to leaving on my business trips now. Once I'm on the plane, it's quiet. There's no one shoving 'to do' lists in my face or asking how much I spent at the grocery store. To tell you the truth, there have been times when I've left a day early, just to get out of the fracas.

183

"I feel like I can never do anything right. I go to the store and spend too much money. I do the laundry and mess it up, which, by the way, only happened twice in the five years that I did it. I cook and Sarah complains that it's overdone, underdone, or something the kids won't eat. We always have to do things the way she wants them done, when she wants them done. It's her way, or there's hell to pay.

"You know, I've just given up. I don't even try anymore. It's never good enough, and I'm tired of this 'I have three kids instead of two' business. If she doesn't think of me as a partner, it's because she doesn't treat me like one.

"My question is, why does she have to be so critical and rigid all the time? If I knew the answer to that, we'd get along much better."

Searching for Common Ground

Although their questions were laced with hurt, anger, and frustration, there was clearly an undercurrent of unmet expectations.

For example, Sarah expected Jack to stop acting irresponsibly, to do his share of the work, and stop being so lackadaisical. She wanted him to act like an adult. Sarah was convinced that if Jack could manage these changes, their relationship would improve significantly.

Jack thought their problems would go away if Sarah would stop being so critical, if she could look for the things he did right, instead of only what was wrong. He also wanted her to relax, slow down, and take some time to do nothing. He was tired of living with a whirling dervish, and he resented that she wanted him to be like her.

By the end of the first few sessions, it was evident that Jack and Sarah were asking the same question, "Why can't my spouse be more like me?"

Their therapist helped them see the answer: fundamental differences in style.

Sarah's style was quick, no-nonsense, hard-charging, and perfectionistic. When something needed to be done, she insisted it be done immediately—or she'd do it herself. She prided herself on getting large amounts of work done in short periods of time. Her friends admired her drive, but said they were glad they didn't have to live with it. She rarely had time to relax, and thought anyone who did was lazy. Patience was not one of her virtues.

Jack's style was less frenetic. He was more deliberate in his decisions. While he made an effort to get things done on time, it was okay if he didn't. He refused to treat missed deadlines or late arrivals as catastrophes. It just wasn't worth it. Jack's motto was, If I don't get it done today, it'll be waiting for me tomorrow. He hated to be rushed.

Jack also hated conflict, and he worked hard to avoid it. When he was confronted, he never knew what to say, so he simply shut down.

At first, Sarah and Jack were disappointed to learn that their marital problems came from their conflicting styles, although they felt relieved that neither of them would have to change their personality. The therapist told them that personality differences could be addressed, and that they could learn how to manage these differences if they were willing to work hard enough.

PROBLEM MANAGEMENT

There are five steps to problem management:
1. Admitting responsibility for the problem
2. Recognizing your contributions to the problem
3. Recognizing the other person's contributions to the problem
4. Knowing what you can control, and what you can't
5. Changing your contributions

Admitting Responsibility

Accepting responsibility for a problem is more difficult for some people than it is for others. Nevertheless, it is an essential step in problem management.

When David went into therapy after his wife left him, he was convinced that their problems were all her fault. "If she wouldn't have gone to medical school, studied so much at the library, and insisted on working with male colleagues, we wouldn't be in this mess."

David couldn't see that his behavior contributed to their marital problems. Having grown up with a violent father, he simply wasn't used to seeing himself as part of the problem. In fact, David considered himself more of a victim when things didn't go his way. During his first few therapy sessions, however, the therapist helped him understand that his behavior had a powerful influence on the people around him and had clearly contributed to Karen's decision to leave.

Sarah and Jack also had trouble admitting responsibility for their problems. Sarah thought they resulted from Jack's laissez-faire attitude, irresponsibility, and unwillingness to grow up. Jack attributed their problems to Sarah's relentless frenzy and insistence that things be done her way. After a few therapy sessions, however, they realized that each of them had contributed to their marital troubles in different ways.

Recognizing Your Contributions

The second step in problem management is to examine *how* we have contributed to the problem. Make a list of your thoughts, feelings, and behaviors that might have triggered or maintained the conflict. Is there anything you have said or done that sparked a negative reaction in the other person? How have you helped maintain an unhealthy pattern of communication? If you can't see how you've contributed to the conflict, think back to comments that other people have made. Maybe a friend has remarked on your problem, or an employer has given you feedback in a performance review. Perhaps your colleague or spouse has expressed concern about your communication style.

David, for instance, was told by various people over the years that his explosions alienated the people around him. This made it difficult for people to approach him, and it accounted for some of the trouble he had in establishing and maintaining relationships.

The therapist asked David to list the attitudes and behaviors that contributed to his problem. Once he identified his contributions, he could focus on changing them. David came up with the following list:

David's Contributions

- The way I express my anger is loud and intimidating.
- I feel threatened by Karen's relationships with other people, especially men.
- I have a hard time listening when other people try to explain their point of view.
- I cut people off when they are talking.
- I lose control if people make decisions I don't like.
- I am impatient.

187

When the therapist first asked Sarah and Jack to make a list of their contributions, Sarah felt irritated. She had no trouble admitting she, was partly responsible for their problems, but having to list specifics made her feel put on the spot. She was afraid that the therapist would think it was all her fault. She felt encouraged, however, by Jack's willingness to make his own list and share it with her in the next session.

Sarah acknowledged that her insistence on having things done her way, along with her irritation with Jack's laid-back style, was a major part of the problem. Jack admitted he was more laid-back than he needed to be sometimes, especially when he was mad at Sarah. While he avoided outright conflict, he wasn't above "getting even" every now and then.

The therapist asked Sarah and Jack to each make a list of their contributions.

Sarah's Contributions

• I make lists of jobs for Jack to do when he gets home from his business trips, and I expect these to be his priority.
• I take over chores when they aren't done the way I want them.
• I get mad if he dawdles when we need to be somewhere on time.
• I let him know when I think he has made a mistake.
• I don't feel like spending time alone with him, because I'm usually so mad about the chores he's not doing.

Jack's Contributions

• I avoid conflict.
• I assume Sarah will take care of things that need to be done around the house.
• I sometimes leave town a day early to get away from the tension.
• I don't call home anymore when I'm on the road, because I don't want to hear the complaints.

Recognizing the Other Person's Contributions

Once you understand your own role in the conflict, it is important to recognize the other person's contributions. The key word here is "recognize." This does not mean finger pointing, blaming, or letting yourself off the hook. You simply acknowledge that the other party shares responsibility for the conflict. This is especially important for individuals who tend to blame themselves or take responsibility for the people around them.

Understanding what we are responsible for, and what we are not, is one of the most important steps in problem management.

Control

Problem management hinges on an understanding of what we can control, and what we cannot. This is an important distinction. We often spend too much time and energy trying to influence other people's behavior instead of changing our own.

As much as we would like to believe in our ability to control the people and events around us, there will always be situations beyond our grasp. Attempting to control other people is a waste of energy. We would do better to learn how to control our own reactions instead.

David, for example, was unable to alter Karen's decision to go to medical school. He felt powerless, angry, resentful, and threatened, and he took every opportunity to let her know. His tirades and threats were ill-fated efforts to control her decisions and change her mind.

Eventually, David discovered that it was *his* behavior that was causing him trouble, not Karen's. In fact, David could choose how to respond to Karen's decisions. He could make threats and throw things around the house, or he could accept her decisions and work through his feelings of jealousy. Clearly, that if he wanted to stay married to Karen, David would need to make fundamentally different choices.

Sarah and Jack were in a similar situation. Sarah was angry, overwhelmed, and frustrated by Jack's apparent indifference to her need for a responsible partner. Jack felt alienated, insulted, and berated. He blamed Sarah for treating him like a child. The more Jack avoided doing things Sarah wanted him to do, the more upset she became. The more upset she became, the more distance he placed between them. As this distance grew, Sarah felt more and more hopeless, so Jack would interact with her even less.

Through therapy, Sarah and Jack realized that they were causing as many problems for themselves as they were for each other. Once they understood this, they could decide what they needed to change about themselves in order to meet the demands of the relationship.

Changing Your Contributions

Once we understand *how* we contribute to our problems, we can design strategies to change or reduce our contributions. This means adopting different ways of thinking, feeling, and behaving.

Change is not something that happens overnight—it takes commitment. We must sustain our efforts over an extended period of time, and when we start to slip (as we all do), we need to pick ourselves up and go forward.

The secret to successful problem management is to address one concern at a time. This can create a domino effect, where the management of one problem can lead to the improvement of another.

Strategies for Managing David's Anger

David's main goal in therapy was to change the way he expressed his anger. First, he considered the situations that made him angry. Then he came up with strategies to use whenever he faced a trigger situation. These strategies would help prevent an angry outburst, allowing him instead to communicate his feelings in a healthy, effective manner.

Strategy One: Put myself on "red alert" when I find myself in a trigger situation.

By identifying risky situations, David could take the time to prepare an appropriate response—and avoid an angry outburst.

Strategy Two: Get information.

After reviewing his list of trigger situations, David realized that he could have responded differently if he had taken the time to get more information.

For instance, if he had asked why an employee refused to work overtime, he might have been perfectly satisfied with the answer. Perhaps the employee had to care for a sick child or go to a funeral. If David had asked why his office furniture was late, he may have learned that the distributor had just filed bankruptcy.

Strategy Three: Don't interrupt!

One of David's biggest problems was his tendency to interrupt other people. To avoid doing this, he resolved to concentrate on what the other person was saying. Then, before he responded, he would ask, "Can I say something now?"

Strategy Four: Don't raise my voice, even if it means I have to stop talking for a minute or two.

If David started to raise his voice, he would take a deep breath and stop talking for a few minutes in order to regain his composure.

Strategy Five: Start sentences with "I."

David knew he had trouble taking responsibility for his anger. As his therapist pointed out, his very sentence structure suggested someone else was to blame. "You make me so mad! Our problems are all your fault."

David resolved to start his sentences with "I," which would make him take responsibility for his feelings and behavior. Instead of saying, "You don't have any clue about how to run a business," David would say, "I'm angry that the furniture is not here."

Managing Style Differences Between Sarah and Jack

The task for Sarah and Jack was to improve their marriage by finding strategies to manage their individual styles.

Before the therapist would work with them, however, Sarah and Jack both had to agree to recommit to the marriage, work hard in therapy, and compromise when necessary.

To start, Sarah and Jack each chose one contribution they were willing to change. Jack selected "I assume Sarah will take care of things that need to be done around the house." Both parties agreed to focus on grocery shopping. Once they selected an area of focus, they were ready to devise problem management strategies.

Strategy One: Make a list.

First, Sarah and Jack agreed to make a grocery list. This may seem like an obvious step, but there were plenty of times when Jack would ask, "What do we need?" and Sarah would get upset, thinking, "He should already know what we need—why do I have to tell him?"

Instead of asking Sarah what they needed, Jack would make a list, then show it to Sarah to see if there was anything she wanted to add.

Both promised to be as specific as possible to avoid confusion. For example, if they needed fruit or meat, they would write down what kind and how much. (This would cut back on the high-priced steaks and other expensive purchases.) Jack would agree to buy what was on the list, but he could add items as he remembered them in the store.

Making a list improved Jack's chances of "getting it right," and Sarah was less likely to get angry.

Strategy Two: Set a deadline.

Sarah agreed to tell Jack when she *needed* the food, which was different from when she *wanted* it. "Right now" was unrealistic—that's how they got into trouble in the first place. "I need it by Sunday night for the kids' lunches," was much more helpful, because Jack could choose when he wanted to shop without any pressure from Sarah.

Strategy Three: Refrain from asking about the cost.

Jack felt like Sarah was looking over his shoulder every time he went shopping. If he was going to shop on a regular basis, he didn't want to get the third degree each time. Sarah promised not to ask about the grocery bill or comment if Jack bought items that weren't on the list.

Strategy Four: Define a time frame.

Sarah and Jack agreed to try these strategies for two months. By establishing a time frame, both parties acknowledged that change doesn't happen overnight. There would be times, especially in the beginning, when they would slip and fall back into their old ways. Sarah and Jack agreed to acknowledge their slipups and get back on board. After two months they would determine if their strategies were successful. If they were still having a conflict over grocery shopping, they would look for new ways to manage their problem.

From her list of contributions, Sarah selected "I get mad if he dawdles when we need to be somewhere on time." This contribution was a significant problem for the couple, because they frequently needed to be somewhere on time, such as church, dinner engagements, doctor appointments, and so forth.

Strategy One: Identify the "real" expected time of arrival and agree on a departure time.

In the past, if their son's soccer game started at 6:30, Sarah would tell Jack it started at 6:00 so they would have enough time to get there. On the rare occasion when they did arrive on time, Jack was angry to discover that they were half an hour early. Lying to Jack didn't do much for Sarah's credibility, and it made Jack even angrier about having to wait. Next time, Jack would dawdle even more, thinking that Sarah had lied about the real time. This only increased Sarah's anger.

To break this cycle, Sarah and Jack called a truce. Sarah agreed not to lie about the real arrival time if she and Jack could compromise on a suitable departure time.

Strategy Two: Refrain from "catastrophizing."

Sarah realized that her concern about being late often started several hours before they had to leave. She was plagued with thoughts like, "It'll be terrible if we're late," "I can't stand to be late because I told my friends I'd be there and I don't want to disappoint them," or "I'm always on time when I'm alone." Her fear of being late affected other activities as well: "I can't play tennis this morning, because we have a wedding to go to tonight and I don't want to be late," "No, you can't stay overnight at your friend's house, because we've been invited out to supper tomorrow and we have to be on time."

Whenever she began to feel anxious, Sarah would repeat to herself, "It's not the end of the world if we're late." By replacing her negative thoughts with something less exacerbating, Sarah would put the importance of a timely arrival into perspective.

Strategy Three: Drive separately.

Although Sarah and Jack agreed to the first two strategies, they were still skeptical. What if Sarah became too anxious about arriving late? What if Jack wasn't ready to go at the time they agreed? They wanted a backup plan.

Sarah agreed to wait ten minutes after the agreed upon departure time. After that, she would let Jack know she was going to drive separately—but there were two conditions. First, Sarah had to tell Jack she was leaving. There would be no sneaking away without telling him or slamming doors on the way out. Second, she could not resent him for not going with her. Leaving was her decision, and she had to take responsibility for it.

THERAPY AND PROBLEM MANAGEMENT

Problem management can be as simple or as intricate as you want. Of course, you can manage problems with or without a therapist, but there are several benefits to working with a therapist.

• A therapist can provide a perspective from outside the eye of the storm. It is difficult to get the whole picture when we're in the middle of chaos.

• Seeing a professional encourages us to follow through on our commitment to change.

• Change often occurs more quickly under professional guidance. A therapist can help identify and break destructive cycles, allowing us to move forward.

• Finally, therapy is a safe place to experiment with change.

Chapter Ten

Pulling It All Together

In many ways, mental health problems have finally emerged from the closet of secrecy and shame. Nevertheless, some people still feel embarrassed about needing and asking for help. This makes it all the more difficult to get accurate information about therapy.

For many clients, it is one thing to call a friend or a nurse help-line and ask questions about rashes, bumps, aches, and pains. It is quite another to call that same help line and request information on depression, anxiety, or family problems.

Some of this reticence is cultural. Asking for help with personal problems is still occasionally seen as a weakness or a character flaw, an indication that we can't cut it on our own.

Most people would not feel ashamed of having to seek treatment for high blood pressure, diabetes, leukemia, multiple sclerosis, or coronary disease. But they go to great lengths to conceal treatment for psychological problems. Some patients fear they will be labeled "crazy" or "unbalanced." They worry that if they are discovered, they will lose credibility, standing in their community, even their livelihood.

In most cases, their fears are unfounded. This is not to say that all communities, employers, friends, or family members are equally enlightened. Pockets of ignorance continue to exist. But acceptance of psychological problems has increased in recent years, due to vigorous education efforts by mental health associations, the public mental health struggles of well-known individuals, and the publication of a number of books and magazine articles related to therapy.

THERAPY IS A PROCESS, NOT A SINGLE EVENT

Therapy is the process of treating a problem that gets in the way of effective living.

> **Process:** 1. A systematic series of actions directed to some end. 2. A specific, continuous action, operation, or series of changes. *(Random House College Dictionary)*

Change is not a cure or a quick fix; it is the result of a series of decisions and actions. Like the potter who adds and subtracts clay to create a well-shaped vase, the individual in therapy experiments with different thoughts, feelings, and behaviors to become the person he or she wishes to be. Throughout the process, the therapist is there to help that individual determine what works and what doesn't.

THERAPY IS A TEAM EFFORT, NOT A SOLO PERFORMANCE

Many patients are under the impression that seeing a mental health professional is like visiting a physician: you tell the doctor what's wrong, and he or she fixes the problem by setting a bone, applying a few well-placed stitches, or prescribing medicine to take the pain away. In most cases, you are the passive recipient of a procedure that is conducted upon you.

This is not the case with psychotherapy. In mental health, it is nearly impossible to treat a patient unless the patient takes an active role in the treatment process.

The therapist is responsible for what happens during the sessions. He or she will help you define your destination, prepare you for the trip, and plot your course of travel.

Your job is to follow your therapist's lead and let him or her know if you are switching destinations. How you travel is up to you: with curiosity, commitment, and effort—or with nonchalance, restraint, and boredom (in which case the trip may be very short, indeed).

THERAPY IS HARD WORK, NOT A WALK IN THE PARK

Therapy is a fascinating process of self-discovery and change. It gives us rare, uninterrupted time to examine ourselves without the ringing of phones, beeping of pagers, clicking of fax machines, or humming of computers. In this way, therapy is a luxury.

But therapy requires commitment and hard work. We must be willing to follow through on appointments, homework assignments, and payments. Hard work comes with honest self-appraisal and effort to change. For most of us, change means trading something comfortable and familiar for something new and maybe a little uncomfortable. Our efforts to change test our motivation, determination, and expectations, but the reward is worth it.

THERAPY IS A MEANS TO AN END, NOT AN END IN ITSELF

Therapy is a tool—a device used to change the parts of our lives that give us trouble. Like all good tools, it is reliable, accessible, and consistent. When we have used it to accomplish our task, the tool goes back on the shelf until it is needed again. It wouldn't make much sense to continue hammering away at a nail that is already in place.

I recently met a psychologist who was treating a woman in her mid-thirties. She had been seeing this patient every week for ten years. They had discussed every major life event that had crossed

200

the client's path during that time: marriages, children, jobs, divorces, friends, parents. When I asked the therapist if she or the client had ever considered terminating treatment, or even taking a break, she asked, "Why?"

In this case, treatment was no longer a tool to be used in the service of a goal. It had become the goal itself.

Therapy serves many functions: to manage problems, improve mood, and increase our ability to carry on from day to day. But one of its primary tasks is to promote independence.

There is nothing wrong with seeking help when help is needed. In fact, one of the hallmarks of maturity is knowing when we need professional help. Seeing a therapist weekly for ten years, however, is more a state of dependence. It becomes difficult for the dependent patient to make decisions without first checking with the therapist. In situations like this, therapy is no longer an adjunct to life, it is the focus of life itself.

Don't get me wrong. Therapy is a very important process, one that should be entered into with serious intentions of self-examination and hard work. Sometimes it's even fun. But when it becomes the focal point of activities over a number of years, it overshadows the real goal—being in the real world, not in therapy.

How you use therapy as a resource is up to you. Work hard, have fun, and enjoy the fruits of your efforts.

BIBLIOGRAPHY

Budman, Simon H. *Forms of Brief Therapy.* New York: Guilford Press, 1981.

Buetler, Larry E.; Paulo P. Machado; and Susan Allstetter Neufeldt. "Therapist Variables." From *Handbook of Psychotherapy and Behavior Change,* edited by Sol Garfield and Allen Bergin. New York: John Wiley & Sons, 1995.

First, Michael B., MD, ed. *Diagnostic and Statistical Manual of Mental Disorders. Fourth Edition.* Washington, D.C.: American Psychiatric Association, 1994.

"Foster Higgens National Survey of Employer-Sponsored Health Plans 1996." New York: A. Foster Higgens Co., 1997.

Garfield, Sol, and Allen Bergin, eds. *Handbook of Psychotherapy and Behavior Change.* New York: John Wiley & Sons, 1995.

Giles, Thomas R. Managed Mental Health Care: *A Guide for Practitioners, Employers.* Boston: Allyn and Bacon, 1993.

St. Paul (Minn.) Pioneer Press, 2 February 1997.

Winegar, Norman. *The Clinician's Guide to Managed Mental Health Care.* New York: Haworth Press, 1992.

INDEX

Kathleen J. Papatola, PhD, graduated from the University of British Columbia, Vancouver, Canada, in 1982. She is a Licensed Psychologist with fifteen years of clinical experience, most of it in managed care. In addition to her clinical work, Dr. Papatola consults with organizations, trains mental health providers, and engages in public speaking. She also writes a regular column for the *St. Paul Pioneer Press'* Opinion Page on current psychological issues.

Dr. Papatola is available to professional and nonprofessional groups for speaking and training engagements. She can be reached at 75764.226@Compuserv.com, or at P.O. Box 40184, St. Paul, Minnesota 55104.